CATHOLIC MORALITY

A Course in Religion
Book III

About This Series

Fr. John Laux, M.A. was a high school religion teacher who distilled the fruit of his many years of research and teaching into these fine high school religion books. At first glance, it might appear foolish to reprint books that were first published in 1928. But a reading of Fr. Laux's books will lay that thought to rest. For he had a rare talent of capsulizing the intricacies of our Catholic Faith and its theology into succinct, precise, learned and yet lively prose, that is at once truly interesting and that all can easily understand. He is profoundly intellectual, yet always clear and easy. His writing, while aimed at the high school student, remains challenging and informative to the college student and the adult Catholic as well. But further, Fr. Laux writes in an undated and almost undateable style, a style that is, one might say, classic and timeless, a style that truly befits his subject matter—the timeless teachings of our Ancient Church. For these reasons, the four books in this high school series are all works of rare genius, as also are his *Introduction to the Bible* and *Church History,* for they all possess these same qualities that make Fr. Laux such a pleasure to read and such a joy to study from.

"Do ye manfully, and let your heart be strengthened,
all ye that hope in the Lord." (Ps. 30, 25)

CATHOLIC MORALITY

SIN, VIRTUE, CONSCIENCE, DUTIES TO GOD,
NEIGHBOR, ETC.

A Course in Religion

For Catholic High Schools and Academies

BOOK III

by

Fr. John Laux, M.A.

Late Instructor of Religion, Notre Dame High School, and Professor of
Psychology, Villa Madonna College, Covington, Ky.

*"And Jesus said to him...Thou knowest
the commandments: Do not commit adultery,
do not kill, do not steal, bear not false witness,
do no fraud, honour thy father and mother."*
—Mark 10:18-19

TAN Books
Charlotte, North Carolina

Nihil Obstat: J. M. Lelen
                    Censor Librorum

Imprimatur: ✠ Francis W. Howard
                    Bishop of Covington, Kentucky
                    March 25, 1932

Library of Congress Catalog Card No.: 90-70439

ISBN 978-0-89555-393-5

Cover illustration: St. John the Baptist awaits beheading.

Printed and bound in India

TAN Books
Charlotte, North Carolina
www.TANBooks.com
1990

A Word to the Teacher

The need of some systematic presentation of the truths of our Holy Religion to boys and girls of our American Catholic High Schools has been felt by Catholic educators for a long time. The manuals now in use have been found to be either too technical or too simple, and the problem has been to prepare a text that would suit the needs of the growing mind, and, while enlisting the interest of the pupils in acquiring a knowledge of religious truths, would at the same time encourage the practice of virtue and cultivate a love for the Church.

The present *Course in Religion for Catholic High Schools and Academies* is an attempt to solve this problem. The general arrangement of the course is based, as far as possible, on the division and order of the larger Baltimore Catechism. The catechetical form of presentation has been abandoned, because, in the opinion of prominent educators, "it is conducive to memory work rather than to reasoning, encourages inefficient teaching, and makes almost no appeal to the interest of the pupil."

For practical purposes the work has been divided into Four Parts, each of which is bound and paged separately and provided with copious helps for study and review, a table of contents and an index.

The First Part embraces the mystery of the Trinity, the work of Creation, Redemption, Sanctification, and Consummation. It is introduced by a brief treatment of the nature, necessity, sources, and qualities of Faith. The Second Part treats of the Means of Grace: the Sacraments, the Sacrifice of the Mass, Indulgences and Sacramentals. Part Three is devoted to General and Special Christian Moral; Part Four to Apologetics.

The writer suggests that every pupil be provided with a copy of the New Testament, to be used throughout the course; a Student's edition of the Missal, to be used in connection with Part Two; and the *Imitation of Christ* as supplementary material for Part Three. It is presupposed that there is a well-stocked Religious Book Shelf in every High School Library.

v

The concluding words of Father Drinkwater's preface to his excellent little book of religious instruction *Twelve and After* are applicable to every textbook in Religion: "Let us remind ourselves that religion is not a book-and-writing matter. Such instruction as this book contains is very useful and in some ways necessary; but there are things even more necessary, such as plenty of singing, corporate prayer, both liturgical and unliturgical, and opportunities for personal service, not to speak of the more individual and interior practice of religion. If these more essential things are well managed, then the intellectual instruction will have all the more meaning and fruit. It should become the raw material of Catholic ideals. We can but build up our altar stone by stone and arrange our wood upon it as carefully as may be, and then pray for the fire of the Lord to fall in acceptance of the offering."

A word to the teacher of religion. The purpose of the teaching of religion must be the same in all our schools from the grades to the university—to form *religious characters,* to train men and women who will be ready to profess their Faith with firm conviction and to practice it in their daily lives in union with the Church.

This obvious purpose of all religious teaching imposes a twofold duty on the teacher of religion in the High School: to give his pupils a *fuller* and *more profound grasp of Christian Doctrine,* and to lead them on to the *intelligent use* of the helps that have been given us to lead Christian lives.

It is idle to dispute, as is sometimes done, whether the training of the intellect is more important than the training of the heart and the will; the imparting of religious knowledge, than the formation of religious habits. Both are of supreme importance. The will follows the intellect; but the intellect is also powerfully influenced by the will. Ignorance may sometimes be bliss, but never in religious matters. Well-instructed Catholics may become backsliders, but their number is small in comparison with those who are lost to the Church because their ignorance of Catholic teaching made them easy victims of the purveyors of false science, shallow philosophy, and neo-pagan morality. Religion requires that the *whole* man worship God with all his faculties and acts. The intellect must *believe* that which is true concerning God—

Faith; and the *will* must be directed to *do* those actions which are right and to avoid those which are wrong—*Morals.*

Catholic Action is toay becoming a vital force throughout the world. The layman cannot effectively engage in Catholic Action unless he is well versed in the teachings of his faith and able at all times to explain and defend it. The type of layman, therefore, that is needed today is the type which Cardinal Newman asked for years ago when he said: "I want laymen, not arrogant, not rash in speech, not disputatious, but men who know their religion, who enter into it, who know just where they stand, who know what they hold and what they do not; who know their Creed so well that they can give an account of it; who know so much of history that they can defend it. I want an intelligent, well instructed laity. I wish you to enlarge your knowledge, to cultivate your reason, to get an insight into the relation of truth to truth; to learn to view things as they are; to understand how faith and reason stand to each other; what are the bases and principles of Catholicism. Ignorance is the root of bitterness."

The great Cardinal's ideal of the Catholic layman may never be fully attained, but it is certainly worth striving after. It is only through such pious and enlightened laymen and laywomen, working with their bishops and pastors, that Catholic Action can be truly successful. It is the chief duty of our Catholic Educational system to place on the battlefield an army of laymen, equipped to "fight the battles of the Lord."

THE AUTHOR.

ACKNOWLEDGMENT

The author and publisher make grateful acknowledgment to P. J. Kenedy & Sons for permission to include copyrighted material from "You and Yours" by Rev. Martin J. Scott, S. J.

CONTENTS

SECTION I

GENERAL MORAL

ix

CATHOLIC MORALITY

A Course in Religion
Book III

St. Ignatius and His Companions Renounce the World

Baumeister

SECTION I

GENERAL MORAL

Introduction

1. God's Will the End of Life

What Is the Meaning and Purpose of Life?—This is the all-important question for every human being; for what will all the world beside profit us if we miss the whole purpose of our existence, if we fail to attain our true destiny?

1. Both reason and revelation tell us that God is the author and the last end of our life. Being creatures of God, the work of His hands, we belong to him absolutely. "In Him we live and move and are" (Acts 17,28). The last end of man can be nothing else but God from whom he came, "for of Him, and by Him, and in Him are all things (Rom. 11,36). Hence the purpose of our life is *to do the will of God,* as it is written in indelible characters in every human heart, as it was proclaimed on Sinai and on the Mount of the Beatitudes, as it is manifested in the duties of our state and calling, and as it is made known to us by those who share in God's authority here on earth in the family, the State and the Church.

But our submission to God's holy will must not be founded on servile fear; it must be a voluntary, loving and generous self-surrender to His will. Our service must be the service of a soldier who unhesitatingly carries out the commands of his general; but also the service of a child that sees in God his loving Father and his greatest benefactor.

2. This ideal of perfect harmony between the human will and the divine will is realized in the life of the *God-Man Jesus Christ.* He came on earth, as He Himself tells us, simply to glorify His Father and to do His will. He speaks of His Father's will as His food and drink, as the atmosphere He breathes, as His unfailing consolation. His whole life from the Crib to the Cross was one act of obedience to His heavenly Father. In His life and death He fulfilled most perfectly what the Angels

I

proclaimed in their Christmas message: "Glory to God in the highest." Hence He could say on the eve of His Passion: "I have glorified Thee on the earth, I have finished My work Thou gavest me to do; and now glorify Thou Me, O Father, with Thyself" (John 17,4).

Christ is, therefore, the bright and shining example for all who seek to attain their life's purpose in its "height and breadth and depth", and thus to lay the foundation of their own *perfect happiness*; for true happiness can be found only in seeking God's honor and glory by doing His will. "God asks no service from us," says a wise and holy man, "which does not promote our highest welfare, and no glory in which we, His creatures, do not share. God seeks His glory in our happiness."

Hence the simple words which we find on the first page of the little Catechism express the highest wisdom: *"We are in this world to do the will of God and thereby to gain everlasting happiness in Heaven."*

2. God's Will the Basis of Morality

1. To give glory to God by doing His holy will: this is the end, the purpose of human life. All our actions should be directed to this end. Every action that brings us nearer to this end is a *good action*; every action, on the other hand, that leads us away from this end, is a *bad action*. Because "only one is good, God" (Mark 10,18), all morality, all moral goodness is based on Him; only that is good which corresponds to His holy will. But God is also the Creator, the Lord of heaven and earth, and therefore He alone can impose His will on mankind, from Him alone comes all moral obligation.

2. That our actions are morally good or morally bad according as they agree or disagree with the divine will, is clearly taught in Scripture. "Not every one that saith to Me, Lord, Lord, shall enter into the Kingdom of Heaven, but he that doth the will of My Father who is in Heaven, he shall enter into the Kingdom of Heaven" (Matt. 7,21). "If thou wilt enter into life," Christ said to the rich young man, "keep the commandments" (Matt. 19,17). For the Son of God Himself the will of God is the rule of life and action. "Did you not know that I must be about My Father's business?" he said to His Mother, who had gently upbraided Him for remaining behind in the temple.

3. For the Apostles, too, the fulfillment of the divine will is the only rule of action. "Be not conformed to this world," St. Paul tells the Romans, "but be ye transformed by the renewing of your mind, so that ye may find out *what is the will of God, what is* good, well-pleasing and perfect" (Rom. 12,2). It is his earnest and unceasing prayer that his converts "may be filled with the knowledge of the will of God, that they may walk worthy of God in all things" (Col. 1,9-10). St. John calls those liars who say they know God, but do not keep His commandments. "But he that keepeth His word, in him in very deed the love of God is perfected" (1 John 2,5).

THE CALL OF CHRIST
"If any man will come after Me, let him deny himself, and take up his cross and follow Me." (Matt. 16, 24)

3. CATHOLIC MORAL SCIENCE

That part of the science of religion which teaches us how to direct our actions to God, our last end, is called *Catholic Ethics* or *Catholic Moral Science*. It is based on Christian principles and draws its conclusions from divine revelation.

As a part of the Christian doctrine—the doctrine of the things we must do, *doctrina faciendorum*—it is confided to the keeping of the Catholic Church. Hence the Catholic Church can, in virtue of the divine assistance granted to her, infallibly define what is good and what is bad, what is permitted and what is forbidden.

The general principles of morality are common to all men; but Christian moral differs essentially from purely natural moral:

a) Christian moral directs man to a *supernatural end*, which can be attained only by supernatural means, based upon faith and grace;

b) It holds out *motives* for right conduct of which unaided reason is either totally ignorant or has only an imperfect knowledge;

c) It establishes most of its conclusions on *divine revelation*, while natural moral derives its principles from the native power of reason alone;

d) It offers *means* of which natural moral knows nothing. Hence Catholic moral is incomparably more sublime, far-reaching, certain, and effectual than merely natural morality. The history of mankind shows that "morality lives by faith and dies by infidelity." "What Greek culture did for the intellect, Christ did for morality: the human race owes its *moral power* to Him" (CHAMBERLAIN).

Catholic Moral is divided into "General" and "Special". General Moral treats of the *conditions of morality* and of *moral good and moral evil*; Special Moral *applies the general principles of morality* to the various circumstances of individual and social life.

The *conditions of morality* are freedom of will, law, and conscience: *freedom* is the *basis*, *law* is the *external*, and *conscience* the *internal norm of morality*.

SUGGESTIONS FOR STUDY AND REVIEW

1. What is the purpose of our life? Briefly explain your answer. How does the *Our Father* answer this question?

2. What kind of submission to God's will should we cultivate? Are we children or slaves of God?

3. Was ever a human will in perfect harmony with the divine will? Would not such a Person be a perfect model for us? Show how the God-Man Jesus Christ is such a model.

4. When are our actions good? When are they bad? Prove your answers from Holy Scripture.

5. What is the science called which teaches us how to direct our actions to God?

6. How is Christian Moral divided? What does each division treat of?

7. What are the *conditions* of morality? If you had no free will, could you perform a *moral act*; that is, an act for which you could be held responsible?

8. *Reading: Imitation of Christ*, Bk. III, ch. 9, "That all things must be referred to God as the final end."

CHAPTER I

Conditions of Morality

A. FREE WILL

1. Nature of Free Will

When the youthful Hercules' education was completed, he set out to seek his fortune. He had not gone far before he met two beautiful women, Kakia (Vice) and Arete (Virtue) by name, who immediately entered into conversation with him. Each offered to be his guide, but bade him choose which he preferred to follow. Kakia promised him riches, ease, honors, and pleasure; Arete warned him that in her wake he would be obliged to wage incessant war against evil, to endure hardships without number, and spend his days in toil and poverty. Silently the hero pondered for a while over these so dissimilar offers, and then, mindful of the instructions he had received, rose from his seat by the wayside, and, turning to Arete, declared himself ready to obey any command she might choose to give him.

This parable is called *Hercules' Choice*: it is an apt illustration of what we mean by *free will*.

1. **Free Will or Moral Freedom** is the power of determining our own acts; the power of acting or not acting, of doing one thing or another as we please. Hercules made use of his free will when he determined to follow Arete; he might have followed Kakia, but he chose to follow Arete.

But *why* did Hercules determine to follow Arete? Both Arete and Kakia presented something *good or desirable* to him and thereby gave him *motives soliciting his will.* He weighed the motives and then made his choice. Free will implies not choice *without* motive, but choice *between* motives. If there is only *one* motive within the range of intellectual vision, the act of the will in such circumstances is not *free*, but *necessary*. A choice without *any* motive would be irrational and impossible (Maher).

2. **Free Will Presupposes Knowledge.**—We are responsible for an action only in so far as we know it to be morally good or bad. Hence we cannot be held responsible for what we do during sleep, in a state of unconsciousness, or during a fit of insanity. Hence, too, children who have not attained the age of discretion are not responsible for their acts. But we must not forget that

5

the seeds of good or bad habits can be sown in earliest childhood. "As the twig is bent, the tree's inclined."

3. We can will only what we know; but our will often influences our intellect. Love and hate, sympathy and antipathy easily darken our understanding and mislead our judgment. The wish is only too frequently the father to the thought, as Shakespeare says; and love is proverbially blind. We readily believe what we *wish* to believe. "He who denies the existence of God," says St. Augustine, "has some reason for *wishing* that God did not exist."

4. **The power to commit sin** does not belong to the essence of moral freedom; for this power presupposes a lack of knowledge: he who sins seeks his happiness in something which is not a real good; he puts a false god in the place of the true God. Hence the more strenuously we combat our evil inclinations and set our mind and will on what is truly good and beautiful, the *freer* we become. "Where the Spirit of God is, there is liberty," says St. Paul (2 Cor. 3,17) ; and Our Lord declares to the Jews: "If you continue in My word, you shall be My disciples indeed, and *you shall know the truth, and the truth shall make you free*" (John 8,31). The blessed in Heaven, who see the Eternal Truth face to face, cannot sin any more.

> The one sole wished-for Good is there,
> And everything defective elsewhere found,
> In it is perfected beyond compare.
> DANTE, *Paradiso,* 33

2. Free Will in the Light of Faith and Reason

1. That man has the power of free choice or free will is clearly taught in Holy Scripture.—Moses said to the children of Israel: "I call Heaven and earth to witness this day, that I have set before you life and death, blessing and cursing: *choose* therefore life" (Deut. 30,19). Everlasting glory is promised to him "who could have transgressed, who could do evil things, and hath not done them" (Eccles. 31,10). Jesus wept over Jerusalem and lamented: "Jerusalem, Jerusalem, how often would I have gathered together thy children, as the hen doth gather her chickens under her wings, and *thou wouldst not*" (Matt. 23,37).

2. The Church has ever championed the freedom of the will against all its opponents.—Against the so-called Reformers of the 16th century, who denied human liberty, the Council of Trent solemnly declared: "If any one says that the free will of man does not co-operate in any way with the grace of God, and that it can not resist the grace of God, but, like a lifeless thing is merely passive, let him be anathema" (Sess. 6, Can. 5-6).

DANTE

7

3. The freedom of the will is also vouched for by the consciousness of each individual and by the common sense of mankind.

a) The very fact that our will acts upon motives; that it waits till it sees a reason for acting; that it passes from one insufficient reason to another till it finds an adequate reason for deciding, proves that it is master of its actions.

b) *Duty, obligation, responsibility, reward,* and *punishment*— words found in the languages, literatures, and laws of all times— all imply *moral freedom.* "If we *ought* to abstain from a forbidden gratification no matter how pleasant it would be to us, if we are to be *responsible* for our deliberate consent to it, if we are *deserving of reward* for resisting it, then assuredly we must be possessed of free will, we must be capable of yielding, just as well as of refusing to yield."

c) All men make a distinction between certain acts done *deliberately* and *freely* and similar acts done *indeliberately.* The whole social system is based on the assumption that the normal person has free will. The state makes laws *for* its citizens. It makes laws *about* animals, not *for* them.

d) The *legal trial* is based on the assumption that man is free and responsible. The fact that the legal trial is to be found in every state in every age, indicates that it is natural for man to believe in free will. If a man can only do what he *must,* if he has no more liberty than a machine, why should he be subjected to trial and punishment? We do not punish an automobile for running over a child, but we do punish a reckless driver.

3. Hindrances to Free Will

1. Free Will is one of God's most splendid gifts to man.— Through his free will man has the wonderful power, unique in all the visible creation, of directing his actions according to his good pleasure. It is this wonderful power that makes him a moral agent, that makes him king and lord of creation, and of all creatures most like to God.

> "Supreme of gifts, which God, creating, gave
> Of His free bounty, sign most evident
> Of goodness, and in His account most prized
> Was *liberty of will*—the boon wherewith
> All intellectual creatures, and them sole,
> He hath endowed."
>
> DANTE, *Paradiso,* 5.

2. Hindrances to Free Will.—But this "supreme gift" of moral freedom is given to us, not as a perfect possession, but as a *power* or *faculty* which we must develop and make as perfect as possible. This task of training and strengthening the will is all the more difficult because of the many obstacles that have to be overcome both from within ourselves and from without.

a) Among the hindrances to free will *concupiscence* takes the first place. By concupiscence we mean the rebellion of our lower against our higher nature, of the flesh against the spirit. Since the fall of our first parents our nature is drawn toward the things of sense, as iron is drawn by the magnet. St. Paul calls this inclination to evil "the law of the members," the law of gravitation, as it were, of our fallen nature, which draws the will down into the sphere of sin, and which cannot be completely and lastingly overcome unless the will of man and the grace of God form an offensive and defensive alliance against it. All merely natural means are insufficient.

Concupiscence lessens our liberty and our responsibility; but if we deliberately excite our passions, we are all the more to blame.

b) Another hindrance to free will is *ignorance*. The exercise of free will presupposes that we *know* what we are doing. We can will only what we know. If we do not know and cannot know that our actions are evil, we do not consent to evil, and cannot be blamed for our actions. In this case our ignorance is said to be *invincible*. But if we suspected that our action was wrong, our ignorance is called *vincible,* and we are to blame for our action; still "the less the knowledge, the less the blame."

c) *Fear* of a grave present or future evil lessens our liberty, but it does not take away our liberty unless it is so intense that we do not know what we are doing; in this case we are not responsible for our actions. A man who perjures himself because he has been threatened with death, is not blameless, but he is less to blame than if he had perjured himself deliberately.

Grave fear, if unjustly caused with a view to bringing marriage about, has always been regarded by the Church as an impediment that makes marriage null and void; it is even probable that this cause nullifies marriage by the natural law.

d) If *violence* is used to make us do wrong, and we refuse our consent, we are not responsible; but if we give partial consent, we are partially to blame. We must remember that only *external acts* can be forced from us; the will as such is beyond the reach of physical violence. The will is an inviolable shrine.

e) Good or bad actions repeatedly performed become *habits,* i.e., we perform them with greater ease, regularity and satisfaction: they become a second nature to us. If we seriously try to overcome bad habits, we disown them, as it were, and any acts that spring from them indeliberately are not really imputable to us.

f) Natural propensities to evil arising from *hereditary taint* lessen the voluntariness of the action just as passion does; but these propensities are not as a rule so strong as to make what in itself is mortally sinful only venial. The struggle against vice is more difficult for those who have inherited some evil propensity, but as long as they are in their right senses they can resist with the help of God's grace, if only they make use of the proper means.

B. LAW

The will of God is the end of life. If we do God's will, we shall infallibly attain our life's purpose—eternal happiness in the possession of God. But how do we know what is the will of God? How is God's will manifested to us? God must have provided some safe and certain rule to direct man's actions towards their last end. That rule we call the *moral law.* It is the means appointed by God by which man may attain his last end.

The will of God, therefore, considered as the rule, norm, or standard of our actions is called *law.* God has revealed Himself as our law-giver in two ways: by the *natural law* and by the *positive divine law.*

1. The Natural Law

The Natural Law is that law which God has written in the heart of man; in other words, it is the light of natural reason by which we discern what is good and what is evil; what is to be done and what is to be left undone; what leads to our last end, and what draws us away from it; what is in accordance with the will of God, and what is contrary to it.

1. That there is such a law is clear from Sacred Scripture.
St. Paul says of the heathens that they "are a law unto themselves", and that they "show that the demands of the law are *written in their hearts,* their conscience bearing witness to them" (Rom. 2,14-15). They are a law to themselves because they

know of themselves what is good and what is evil; reason is to them the herald of the eternal law of God.

The *pagans* themselves bear witness to the truth of the words of St. Paul. Socrates declared before the judges who condemned him to death that he would rather give up liberty and life itself than become a traitor to the dictates of the moral law. In his oration *pro Milone* Cicero says: "There exists a genuine and absolute law, right reason conformed to nature, universal, unchangeable, eternal, whose voice teaches us the good it commands, and turns us away from the evil it forbids. To ignore it is to trample under foot one's very nature, and to inflict upon oneself by that alone the most cruel punishment, even though one should escape all the chastisements imposed by human justice." Juvenal, the Roman satirist, echoes these words when he says: "By the verdict of his own breast no guilty man is ever acquitted."

The superiority of the unwritten moral law over all man-made laws is beautifully expressed by Sophocles, the greatest dramatist of antiquity. Against the command of her uncle, King Creon of Thebes, Antigone buries the body of her brother Polynices. She is caught in the act and brought before the king:

> *Creon* (to Antigone). Knew'st thou our edict that forbade this thing?
> *Antigone.* I could not fail to know. You made it plain.
> *Creon.* How durst thou then transgress the published law?
> *Antigone.* I thought not thy commandment of such might
> That one who is mortal thus could overbear
> The *infallible, unwritten laws of Heaven.*
> Not now or yesterday they have their being,
> But everlastingly, and none can tell
> The hour that saw their birth. I would not, I,
> For any terror of a man's resolve,
> Incur the God-inflicted penalty
> Of doing them wrong.
> *Antigone* transl. by CAMPBELL.

"Two things," says Kant, "fill the soul with an ever renewed admiration and reverence: the starry heavens above me, and the immutable prescriptions of the moral law within me."

2. The subject-matter of the natural law is: (*a*) the primary precepts of morality, (*b*) the immediate conclusions, and, (*c*) the remote conclusions drawn from the primary precepts.

a) There are *three primary precepts of morality* corresponding to man's relation to God, to himself, and to his neighbor: We should worship God, we should control our sensual appetites, we should not do to others what we would not have them do to us.

A fourth might be added: Thou shalt honor thy father and thy mother. No normal person can be ignorant of these fundamental principles.

b) The *immediate conclusions* from these primary precepts are the *Ten Commandments,* with the exception of the Third. These conclusions are reached by a process of reasoning so simple as to be within the powers of the most illiterate.

c) In regard to the *remote conclusions,* such as the indissolubility of marriage, the unlawfulness of private revenge for bloodshed, and the like, ignorance is possible and excusable.

3. The natural law is the foundation of all other laws.— Every law that contradicts the natural law is unjust and not binding in conscience. Since the natural law flows from the Eternal Law, that is, from the Divine Reason and Will, it is *binding on all men* independently of time or place or circumstances; it cannot be abrogated, nor can any part of it be changed, nor can any one be dispensed from it. There is no double standard of morality, one for the strong and another for the weak, one for the rich and another for the poor, one for the learned and another for the unlearned, one for the superior and another for the inferior.

4. But may not God, the Author of the natural law, change it if He so desires? May He not dispense anyone whom He may choose to dispense? We answer: To say that God could change the natural law or dispense from it, would imply that God could contradict Himself, would imply that certain actions were good or bad simply because He commanded or forbade them, and not that He commanded or forbade them because they were *intrinsically,* that is, in themselves, of their very nature, good or bad.

2. The Positive Divine Law

More clearly and fully than by the Natural Law God has made His will known by supernatural revelation, especially in the Old and New Testaments. This revealed law is called the *Divine Positive Law.*

1. Divine positive laws are necessary to man (*a*) in order to explain the natural law, especially those parts of it which are not so readily known and understood by reason alone; (*b*) because God gave man a supernatural destiny and therefore had to regulate man's actions so that he might be able to attain that destiny.

2. The divine positive law is divided into the *Law of the Old* and the *Law of the New Testament;* or simply, into the

Old and the *New Law.* The *Old Law* is subdivided into (*a*) the *Patriarchal* and (*b*) the *Mosaic Law.*

a) Even before the Fall God gave a positive law to our first parents: "Of the tree of knowledge of good and evil thou shalt not eat" (Gen. 2,8). After the Fall He imposed the *Law of Labor* on mankind: "In the sweat of thy face thou shalt eat bread till thou return to the earth out of which thou wast taken" (Gen. 3,19). To Noe and his sons He said after the Deluge: "Flesh with blood thou shalt not eat. Whosoever shall shed man's blood, his blood shall be shed" (Gen. 9,4-6). On the children of Israel He laid the law of Circumcision.

b) The Mosaic Law is divided into *ceremonial, judicial,* and *moral* precepts. The ceremonial precepts had reference to the system of religious worship established by God under the Old Law; the judicial regulated the civil government of the chosen people, and when the old dispensation gave place to the new at the coming of Christ both ceased to have binding force. But Christ by no means abolished the moral precepts contained in the Mosaic Law; on the contrary, He set His seal upon them, perfected them and promulgated them anew for all time. "Do not think," He said, "that I am come to destroy the law or the prophets. I am not come to destroy, but to fulfill" (Matt. 5,17).

3. The New Law.—In the Sermon on the Mount Jesus, the Lawgiver of the New Testament, emphasized the necessity of the inward holiness and corrected some false interpretations of the Old Law, which were current among the Jews of His time. He developed what was implicitly contained in the moral precepts of the Decalogue (Ten Commandments), and He added to the precepts *Counsels of Perfection,* which He proposed as the ideal of the Christian life. He calls His commandment of love new, not because that great commandment did not bind under the Old Law, but because He urged it anew, gave us new motives to practice it, especially His own divine example and wish.

The only really new moral precepts found in the New Law are such as follow from the truths which Christ made known to us, and from the institution of the Sacraments. We are under moral obligation to believe explicitly in the Blessed Trinity, the Incarnation, and the other articles of the Christian faith, and to receive Baptism, the Holy Eucharist, and the other Sacraments instituted by Christ (Slater).

Hoet

THE LAW OF THE OLD TESTAMENT
The Giving of the Ten Commandments

Schumacher

THE LAW OF THE NEW TESTAMENT
The Sermon on the Mount

3. Human Positive Laws

In order that the divine law may be made known to men till the end of time and applied to suit the changing conditions of time and place, the Eternal Lawgiver has appointed representatives among men and given them a share in His legislative power. Hence the power exercised by parents over their children and by the Church and the State over their subjects comes from God; it is a participation in the divine authority.

1. Parental authority is expressly proclaimed in the Fourth Commandment. It embraces the whole life of the child. Its object is the corporal and intellectual, the temporal and eternal welfare of the child.

2. The Catholic Church has received from her divine Founder full and independent authority to make laws binding on all her children in matters which pertain to religion and the salvation of souls. "Whatsoever you shall bind upon earth, shall be bound also in Heaven" (Matt. 18,18). The Apostles knew that they possessed this power and exercised it. At the Council of Jerusalem they solemnly declared: "It hath seemed good to the Holy Ghost and to us, to lay no further burden upon you than these necessary things . . ." (Acts 15,28).

The laws of the Church bind only those who have been baptized. One who has been validly baptized, but belongs to a non-Catholic denomination, is strictly speaking, bound to observe the laws of the Church, but he is as a matter of fact dispensed from them as long as he remains in error without any fault of his.

3. Scripture teaches most clearly that the power of the State to make laws is also derived from God.—In a public interview Christ told the Jews: "Render to Caesar the things that are Caesar's" (Matt. 22,31). Obedience to the civil authority, to an edict of the Emperor Augustus, marks the beginning of Christ's earthly life, and one of His last utterances concerned the divine origin of all human authority. "Thou shouldst not have any power against Me," He said to Pilate, "unless it were given thee from above" (John 19,10).

St. Peter echoes the words of Christ: "Fear God; honor the king . . ." and St. Paul says: "Let every soul be subject to the higher authorities; for there is no authority that is not from God, and the existing authorities are appointed by God. Wherefore he

"Amen I say to you, whatsoever you shall bind upon earth,
shall be bound also in heaven; and whatsoever you shall loose
upon earth, shall be loosed also in heaven." (Matt. 18, 18)

Ciseri

"Render therefore to Cæsar the things that are Cæsar's;
and to God, the things that are God's." (Matt. 22, 21)

that opposeth the authorities resisteth the ordinance of God; and they that resist shall bring upon themselves a judgment" (Rom. 13,1-3).

C. CONSCIENCE

Law is the expression of God's will. It is the external norm or rule of our actions. It is by knowing and *applying* law to our individual actions that we attain our final end. This is done by *Conscience*.

1. Conscience, therefore, is the connecting link between law and particular acts.—It is the *application* of the natural law to our thoughts, words, and deeds. It is the *judgment* passed by our reason on the moral worth of our actions already done, being done, or to be done in the future.

The process by which we arrive at this judgment is as follows: Our mind recognizes the primary principles of the natural law as true and binding on all; our mind also knows the conclusions drawn from these principles; our conscience applies this knowledge to a particular act. For example, the natural law tells me that evil must be avoided and that theft is an evil act; from these premises my conscience concludes: Therefore it is not lawful for thee to make off with this hat or this pair of shoes which belongs to another.

When there is question of obeying a positive law our conscience is formed as follows: I must obey all who command me with lawful authority. The Church commands me with lawful authority to receive Holy Communion at Easter time or to abstain from meat on Fridays. Therefore I must receive Holy Communion at Easter time and abstain from meat on Fridays. The drawing of this conclusion, or the conclusion itself, is called the *dictate of conscience*.

2. We do not need to prove that we have a conscience.—All who have the use of reason *know that they have a conscience.* "Let no one," says St. John Chrysostom, "pretend to ascribe the neglect of virtue to ignorance or say he has no guide or no one to show the way. We have a competent teacher, namely, *conscience*, of whose aid no one is deprived. For the knowledge of what is to be done and what is to be left undone is in man *from the day in which he is formed.*"

The deepest well-spring of conscience is, therefore, God Himself, the Author of our nature. In our conscience He manifests Himself as our *Lawgiver* and our *Judge*: as our Lawgiver who commands or forbids an act; as our Judge who after the act has been done decides whether it deserves blame or praise, punishment or reward. Hence conscience is justly called the *voice of God* in man.

Schnorr

Adam and Eve, stricken in conscience, try to hide from God

3. The word conscience does not occur in the Old Testament or in the Gospels. In its place Our Lord uses the words *heart* and *interior light*. "A good man out of the good treasure of his heart bringeth forth that which is good, and an evil man out of the evil treasure bringeth forth that which is evil; for out of the abundance of the heart the mouth speaketh" (Luke 6,4). The heart, that is, the conscience, is according to Christ, the birthplace of good and evil. In a striking similitude He shows the necessity and the importance of conscience for morality: "The light of thy body is thy eye. If thy eye be single thy whole body shall be lightsome. If then *the light that is in thee* be darkness, the darkness itself how great shall it be?" (Matt. 6,22-23). What the eye is for our body, the interior light is for our moral life. Where this light does not shine, there is no morality, nor good nor evil; all is darkness and night. But by the bright flame of the interior light we see the way which we must go, the pitfalls and obstacles and dangers which we must avoid.

St. Paul introduced the word conscience into the Christian vocabulary. He found it in use both among the Greeks and the Romans (Gr. *suneidesis*, Lat. *conscientia*). He tells us that it forms a part of every man's moral equipment. "The gentiles," he says, "show the work of the law written in their hearts, their *conscience* bearing witness to them" (Rom. 2,15).

But St. Paul not only introduced the word conscience into the Christian vocabulary, he also gave it a Christian meaning: the conscience of the Christian is a *conscience whose rule and standard is the will of God.* Our conscience can err—there is such a thing as an erroneous conscience—but if the will of God is the measure of our conscience, if we form our conscience "in Christ and in the Holy Ghost," it is an infallible guide of right conduct. "I speak the truth *in Christ, I lie not, my conscience bearing me witness in the Holy Ghost*" (Rom. 9,1).

4. We distinguish several kinds of conscience.—

a) A *true conscience* speaks the truth; it tells what is truly right and truly wrong. It is a genuine Echo of the voice of God.

b) A *false or erroneous conscience* tells us that something that is really wrong is right, and something that is really right is wrong. We may be to blame for this error or not; if we are to blame, our conscience is said to be *culpably erroneous*; if we are not to blame, it is said to be *inculpably erroneous.*

c) If our conscience, whether it speaks the truth or not, speaks with assurance, without a suspicion of error, and its voice carries conviction, we are said to have a *certain conscience.*

d) If our conscience has nothing definite to tell us about the goodness or badness of an action, it is called a *dubious* or *doubtful conscience.* To doubt is to suspend judgment. Hence a doubtful conscience is one that does not function.

5. We are always bound to follow a certain conscience,

even if false or erroneous. "All that is not from conscience," says St. Paul, "is sin" (Rom. 14,23). The reason is clear. We are judged by God according as we do good or evil. Our merit or demerit is dependent on our responsibility. We are responsible only for the good or evil we *know* we do. But knowledge and certainty come from a certain conscience. Therefore, if we disobey a certain conscience, we make ourselves responsible. A Protestant who is fully convinced that it is a sin to hear Mass or to speak to a priest would undoubtedly commit sin by so doing.

No authority, ecclesiastical or civil, can make it lawful for us to do what our conscience condemns as *certainly wicked.* "God Himself can not make it lawful for a man to act against his own conscience, because to do so without sin is a contradiction in terms."

6. We are never allowed to act with a doubtful conscience.

—We must clear up the doubt before acting. I am uncertain, for example, whether a person has paid me a debt which he owed me. May I while in this frame of mind exact payment from him? Certainly not; for in this case I would be equally as ready to do wrong as right.

We are bound to *form our conscience* with great care. If we have serious grounds for suspecting that our conscience is erroneous, we are strictly obliged to look well into the matter. We are bound to take all reasonable means, such as good and honest people do take when there is danger of offending God. We ought to pray for light and consult others, who are more learned or prudent than we are. If after that our ignorance cannot be overcome, it is plain that we are not responsible for the error into which we have fallen.

7. The best means for cultivating and perfecting our conscience are —

a) To practice *truthfulness* in word and deed;

b) To *repress* those passions which tend to stifle the voice of conscience, especially *pride* and *impurity*;

c) To *examine our conscience* every evening before retiring to rest;

d) To go to *confession* frequently;

e) To make a *retreat* from time to time.

On the excellent fruits of daily self-examination Benjamin Franklin writes in his *Autobiography*: "Conceiving that daily examination would be necessary, I contrived the following method for conducting that examination. I made a little book, ruling each page so as to have seven columns, one for each day of the week, marking each column with a letter for the day. I crossed these columns with thirteen red lines, marking the beginning of each line with the first letter of one of the virtues, on which line, and in its proper column, I might mark by a little black spot every fault I found upon examination to have been committed respecting that virtue upon that day. . . . Conceiving God to be the fountain of wisdom, I thought it right and necessary to solicit His assistance for obtaining it; to this end I formed the little prayer, which was prefixed to my tables of examination for daily use. . . . I entered upon the execution of this plan for self-examination, and continued if with occasional intermissions for some time. I was surprised to find myself s much fuller of faults than I had imagined, but I had the satisfaction of seeing them diminish. I was often almost ready to give up the attempt . . . for something that pretended to be reason was every now and then suggesting to me that such extreme nicety as I exacted of myself might be a kind of foppery in morals. . . . But, on the whole, tho' I never arrived at the perfection I had been so ambitious of obtaining, but fell far short of it, yet I was by the endeavor a better and a happier man than I otherwise should have been if I had not attempted it."

By making use of these natural and supernatural means we shall secure for ourselves the inestimable blessing of a *true conscience,* whose judgment is always in accordance with the will of God; of a *watchful conscience,* which detects and signals the approach of evil, no matter under what disguise it may appear; of a *tender conscience,* which fears to offend God in the slightest degree; and we shall thus build up in our hearts a kingdom of peace and joy.

"In this I myself also endeavor to have always a conscience, without offense towards God and towards men" (St. Paul, Acts 24,16).

"Have a good conscience and thou shalt ever have joy" (*Imitation of Christ,* II, 6).

D. COLLISION OF RIGHTS AND DUTIES

Christ commanded His Apostles to preach the Gospel. The Sanhedrin "charged them not to speak at all, nor to teach in the name of Jesus." The Apostles decided that they "ought to obey God rather than men," and continued to announce the good tidings of salvation in spite of threats and scourging and imprisonment.

This example shows us what is meant by *collision of rights and duties.* We are sometimes confronted by two laws which we can not observe at the same time. Which one must be obeyed? The decision is not always easy. We have to care for our temporal as well as our eternal welfare, for the needs of our body as well as for the needs of our soul; we do not live for ourselves only, but we are also members of society; we have duties towards God and towards our neighbor, to our Church and to our country. Which of these duties takes precedence?

To answer this question we must remember that there is never any *real,* but only an *apparent* collision of rights and duties. "No man can serve two masters." The will of God, which cannot contradict itself nor demand what is impossible, never binds any of His creatures to observe two conflicting laws at the same time. In every case the lesser law must give place to the greater, the lower right or duty to the higher. Hence.

a) The *Natural Law takes precedence of any Positive Law.* I am allowed to work on Sundays in order to help some one in need, or to miss Mass in order to wait on a sick person;

b) The *Divine Law takes precedence of any Human Law.* We are never allowed to obey a human law if it commands something sinful; the martyrs disobeyed the Roman law which commanded them to sacrifice to idols.

c) The *claims of justice are higher than the claims of charity.* I must pay my debts before giving money to a charitable cause;

d) *Duties to which I am bound by my profession are higher than mere personal duties.* A policeman, a fireman, a doctor, a nurse, must run the risk of personal injury to health or life in order to save others.

e) The *salvation of our souls is a higher duty than the preservation of our life.* We cannot deny our faith in order to escape death.

SUGGESTIONS FOR STUDY AND REVIEW

A. Free Will

1. Show from the story of *Hercules' Choice* what we mean by Free Will. What is a *motive*? Can you act without a motive? Why do we say: "Free Will implies a choice between motives"? Give an example.
2. "Free Will presupposes knowledge." Explain this statement.
3. "Our will often influences our intellect." Explain this statement.
4. What does Holy Scripture say about Free Will?
5. What has the Church always taught about Free Will?
6. How can you prove that you have a Free Will?
7. Why is Free Will such a splendid gift of God to man?
8. Why must we train and strengthen our will?
9. Which is the chief hindrance to the exercise of our Free Will? How can we overcome this hindrance?
10. Name and briefly explain some other hindrances to Free Will. Can any one force you to commit sin? Why not?
11. "*Albert* neglected his studies when he was a medical student. In spite of warnings from professors and parents, he gave a great deal of time to amusements of all sorts. He managed to pass his examinations, but there were some important subjects of which he was ignorant. When he began to practice medicine, he soon found out his deficiencies. His prescriptions seemed to do more harm than good."

    Is Albert responsible for the harm he does to his patients? Is his ignorance *vincible* or *invincible*? What must he do before he may be permitted to continue his practice of medicine?
12. *What is a Human Act?*—"When a man acts without a purpose, can we call his act a human act? No. Because he does not bring into play

those very faculties, intelligence and free will, which characterize him as a human being.

"What, then, do you call an act performed without a purpose; that is, performed without intelligence and free will?

"It is called simply an *act of the man*, but not a *human act*. This is the case whenever either knowledge or free will is wanting. Thus, when persons walk in their sleep, they do not perform human acts, because they do not *know* what they are doing. On the other hand, a person may stumble and fall. *He* really falls. He knows at the time that *he* is falling, but the *falling* is not the result of his free will; it is against his will. The act is not a human act. Again, a person may drink poison, thinking it to be pure water. He knows that he is drinking, and he drinks of his own free will. In so far, therefore, as the mere drinking is concerned, there may be said to be a human act. But he neither knows that he is *drinking poison*, nor does he will to *drink poison*. Hence his *drinking poison* is not a human act. He knows and wills the *drinking*, but not the *drinking poison*" (POLAND, S.J., *Fundamental Ethics*, Chicago: Loyola University Press, p. 12).

B. LAW

1. The Natural Law

1. How does God make known His will to us?
2. What do we understand by the Natural Law?
3. Prove that such a law exists. What other names are given to it?
4. What is the subject-matter of the Natural Law?
5. What are the three primary precepts of morality; that is, those precepts of which no normal person can be ignorant?
6. Which are the immediate conclusions from these primary precepts? Show how each of the Ten Commandments, except the Third, is a conclusion from one or other of the primary principles of morality. For example: "Thou shalt not bear false witness against thy neighbor" is a conclusion from the third primary precept: We should not do to others what we would not have them do to us.
7. A Roman law commanded all Roman subjects to offer sacrifice to the statues of the Roman emperors. Why was this law unjust and not binding in conscience?
8. Why cannot even God change the Natural Law or dispense from it?

2. The Positive Divine Law

1. What do we understand by a positive law? By a positive divine law?
2. Why are positive divine laws necessary to men?
3. How are the positive divine laws divided?
4. Give some examples of positive divine laws before Moses.
5. Which Mosaic Laws are no longer binding? Which Mosaic Laws did Christ perfect and confirm for all times?
6. Why is Christ called the Lawgiver of the New Testament?

7. Why did Christ call the commandment of love *His* commandment and a *new* commandment?
8. Which new moral precepts are found in the New Law? Would we be transgressing a command of Christ if we did not believe in the Mystery of the Blessed Trinity, or if we did not receive Holy Communion?

3. Human Positive Laws

1. Why are human positive laws necessary? Give examples.
2. Show that parents, the Church, and the State have been authorized by God to make laws.
3. Who is bound by the laws of the Church?

C. CONSCIENCE

1. What do we mean by Conscience?
2. How do we arrive at the "dictate of conscience"? Give an example.
3. Is the word conscience found in the Gospels? What words does Our Lord use for conscience?
4. What does St. Paul teach about conscience?
5. Why do we not need to prove that we have a conscience?
6. How does God manifest Himself in our conscience?
7. Distinguish and illustrate four kinds of conscience.
8. What kind of conscience must we always follow? Give an example.
9. Are we allowed to act with a doubtful conscience?
10. Which are the best means of cultivating and perfecting our conscience?
11. The Venerable Thomas à Kempis says: "Have a good conscience and thou shalt ever have joy." Comment on these words.
12. *Conscience the Interpreter of the Moral Law.*—"Implanted in us is a Moral Law whose incorruptible interpreter is Conscience. Of this I am as well aware as of my own existence. This monitor is, to some extent, innate in all men. The lowest member of the human race has *some* intuitive knowledge of the difference between right and wrong; and there is in him an instinctive feeling of obligation to do the former, rather than the latter. However callous criminals become, that inward voice still speaks within them; and after committing murder, deeds of excessive cruelty, and acts of base ingratitude, they are conscious of guilt.

     "This monitor does not entreat or argue with us; it *commands.* It says imperiously: 'This is right, that is wrong; do the former, do not do the latter.' As a free agent, I can disobey its mandate, but, though I do so, I well know I *ought* to have obeyed it."—STODDARD, *Rebuilding a Lost Faith.* (New York: P. J. Kenedy & Sons) p. 43.
13. We are sometimes confronted by two laws which we cannot observe at the same time. Which one must we obey? Illustrate your answer with examples.

CHAPTER II

Moral Good

1. Elements of a Moral Act

1. A human act is morally good if its *object*, its *circumstances*, and its *end* are good; if any of these is bad, the act is morally evil. Thus almsgiving is something good in itself, but may be bad in certain circumstances, and is always bad if prompted by a bad motive.

2. The Object.—The moral goodness of an act depends, in the first place, on the *object*, that is, the thing to which the act is directed. Almsgiving is morally good, because it is good in itself, or conformable to the divine will; theft is morally evil, because it is evil in itself, contrary to the divine order and the natural law.

In the case of an *erroneous conscience* the morality of an action, as we have seen above, does not depend upon the object *as it is in itself*, but *as it is represented by the mind*.

If the object is in itself *morally indifferent*, such as whistling or walking, the *act* of whistling or walking may be good or bad according to the intention. An individual, deliberate act cannot be morally indifferent.

3. The Circumstances.—*Circumstances* are certain accidental conditions which modify the act in some external way. Just as color or weight or strength or weakness renders a thing better or worse, good or bad in the physical order, so also are human acts affected for better or worse by the circumstances of person, time, place, quantity, and so forth. The circumstances of an action are summed up in the following line:

Who, what, where, when, by what means, why, and how?

Who?—A superior or subject, a priest or layman? Si duo faciunt idem, non est idem.

What?—A smaller or larger quantity of money stolen, an ordinary drinking cup or a consecrated chalice?

Where?—In a church?

When?—On a Sunday?

By what means?—Sinful means?

Why?—Murder committed with the intention of robbery.
How?—Deliberately or indeliberately?

4. The End.—Every reasonable being has an *end* in view when he acts. He acts from a motive or purpose. Without it the will would never be moved to act. It is clear that the end or motive which induces us to act holds the most prominent place among the sources of the morality of our acts.

The best motive is the honor and glory of God. Such a motive makes even morally indifferent acts pleasing to God. "Whether you eat or drink or whatsoever else you do, do all to the glory of God" (1 Cor. 10,31).

Christian motives for acting are: fear, hope, obedience, gratitude, and love. The highest of these is *love,* because love is the complete surrender of ourselves to God. But fear is also a permissible motive; not servile or slavish fear, but filial fear which is never without at least the beginning of love. "Piety," says St. Augustine, "begins with fear and ends in love."

5. A good motive or intention cannot make a bad action good.—Evil must never be done that good may come of it. This is the teaching of Holy Scripture and of the Catholic Church. "Let us not do evil," says St. Paul, "that there may come good" (Rom. 3,8). According to Pope Innocent III it is not lawful to tell a lie even to save another's life.

The Jesuits have been falsely accused of teaching that the end justifies the means. Father Dasbach, editor of a German Catholic paper, promised to give anyone a thousand dollars who would prove in open court that the Jesuits had ever taught this doctrine. An ex-Jesuit undertook to do so, but he failed in his suit when it was tried in Cologne in 1905.

6. It may be asked: Is it lawful to perform an action which produces two effects, one good, the other bad?—

We answer: Such an act is permissible under the following conditions:

a) The action, viewed in itself, must be good, or at least indifferent;

b) The evil effect must not be intended, but only permitted;

c) There must be a sufficiently weighty reason for permitting the evil effect;

d) The good effect must follow at least as immediately as the evil one;

e) The good effect must outweigh the evil.

Hence if I am attacked by a man whose clear intention is to take my life, and if I realize that the only way to save my life is to take his, I am justified in doing so. All the conditions required to justify my act are present.

2. VIRTUE, OR MORAL GOOD AS A HABIT

1. What Is Virtue?—A person who only performs an occasional good act cannot be called good; to deserve that name he must perform good acts regularly; in other words, the performance of good acts must have become a habit, a second nature. Such a good habit is called *virtue*.

Virtue may, therefore, be defined as a *firm and permanent disposition to perform good acts*. Virtue renders our good actions easier, more pleasant and more perfect.

The word *virtue* comes from the Latin *vir*, man, signifying something strong, manly, virile. For the Roman virtue meant manliness and energy in action. Meekness, humility, self-denial had no place in the pagan list of virtues. Christ laid as much stress on suffering and self-denial as on energetic action. "Learn of Me," He said, "because I am meek and humble of heart."

2. Division of Virtue.—Since we have both a natural and a supernatural life, we divide virtues into *natural* and *supernatural* according as they belong to the order of grace, or not.

Natural virtues are the result of good actions frequently repeated. All Christian virtues are supernatural. We cannot acquire them unless God *disposes our souls in a special manner*. This He does by implanting these virtues, like so many seeds, together with sanctifying grace in the soul in Baptism. But these *infused virtues*, as they are called, will not grow and prosper unless, with the help of God's grace, we cultivate them, and cultivation means constant practice.

According to their *object* the Christian virtues are divided into *theological* (or divine) virtues and *moral* virtues. The theological (Greek *theos*, God) have God for their immediate object; the moral virtues, some created thing which may serve as a means for arriving at God, our last end. We shall speak of the theological virtues when we treat of our duties to God. The moral virtues regulate our relations to our fellow-men and to all creatures and therefore properly belong to Special Moral, but for obvious reasons it is well to consider them separately.

Führich

"Learn of Me, because I am meek and
humble of heart." (Matt. 11, 29)

3. The Moral Virtues

1. The numerous moral virtues, by which our whole moral life is regulated and dominated, can be reduced to four fundamental ones: *Prudence, Justice, Temperance,* and *Fortitude.* These are called the Cardinal Virtues because all the other moral virtues are included in them and turn on them, as a door on its hinges (Latin *cardo,* a hinge). Prudence regulates our *reason,* Justice our *will,* Temperance and Fortitude our *sensual appetites.*

Many pagan philosophers, such as Socrates, Plato, and Cicero, had a clear knowledge of the cardinal virtues. Plato assigns to them the primacy in his Ideal State, and Cicero deduces all the other virtues from them. They are mentioned repeatedly in Holy Scripture. The Book of Wisdom (8,7) says that "temperance, prudence, justice, and fortitude are the most profitable things in life."

2. We are prudent if in all our actions we bear in mind our true end, namely, the possession of God in Heaven, and choose the right means to attain it.

Prudence is so necessary that without it no virtue is possible. St. Aloysius was prudent, because he was guided in all his actions by the thought: "What will this profit me for eternity?"

3. We are just if we give to every one his due—*suum cuique* —and do not interfere with his rights. Whoever practices this virtue observes the whole moral law.

We all owe something to God, to our parents and country, to all legitimate superiors, to benefactors, to friends and enemies, to the sick and the poor. Hence no one can be called just who is not religious, pious, obedient, grateful, kind, merciful, truthful, and so on. In Holy Scripture a just man is one who observes the whole law of God. Christ identifies justice with holiness: "Blessed are they that hunger and thirst after justice" (Matt. 10,16).

4. We are temperate if we check our sensual appetites. Temperance has been called "the balance wheel of man's moral life." It moderates our desires and keeps them within the bounds of reason. It is reasonable to use whatever God has created, but we must use all creatures according to their natural ends and God's express law.

Not sensual appetite, but reason must rule in us. "Dearly beloved," writes St. Peter, "I beseech you as strangers and pilgrims, to refrain yourselves from carnal desires which war against the soul" (1 Pet. 2,11).

We speak of the "golden mean," and the old adage says: *In medio stat virtus,* virtue stands in the middle. "Avoid all excess," is a saying ascribed to Solon, the Athenian lawgiver and one of the Seven Wise Men of Greece.

In order to be truly temperate a number of other virtues are necessary: *chastity,* which subjects sexual desires to the law of reason; *humility,* which moderates the estimation of our own importance; *meekness,* which restrains anger; *clemency,* which keeps punishment within reason; *modesty,* which does the same for conduct and dress; *moderation in study,* which tempers our passion for knowledge that "puffeth up," as St. Paul says.

5. We possess fortitude when neither hardship nor persecution can make us shrink from the practice of virtue. Fortitude has been called "a medium between rashness and fear." It manifests

Schnorr

FORTITUDE
The Martyrdom of the Machabees

itself especially in dangers that threaten life; its most beautiful
flower is martyrdom. The Acts of the great martyr St. Lawrence
tell us that "the fire which burned in his soul was stronger than
that which consumed his body."

Allied to fortitude are: *Magnanimity*, or greatness of soul,
which inclines us to heroic acts of virtue; *patience*, which prevents
us from sinking under the weight of affliction; *perseverance*, which
pursues a good cause to the end, despite all obstacles.

Horace pays a fine tribute to the strong and upright man: "Not the
rage of the rabble pressing to hurtful measures, not the aspect of a threat-
ening tyrant can shake from his settled purpose the man who is upright
and determined in his resolution . . . if a crushed world should fall in
upon him, the ruins would strike him undismayed" (*Carm.* III, 3).

4. CHRISTIAN PERFECTION

1. The Perfect Christian.—It must be the aim of the Christian to practice not merely one or the other virtue, but all the virtues of his state of life, and to practice them to as high a degree as
possible and *for the love of God*. If he does this he is said to be a

perfect Christian. Christian perfection, therefore, consists in this: *that we love God above all, and all in God.*

2. Now since the measure of the love of God, as St. Bernard says, is *love above all measure,* Christian perfection is an *ideal* which all men without exception must strive to attain, but which can never be fully attained in this world. As long as we are pilgrims here below, perfection is, for the best and holiest, something incomplete, a constant, restless striving after the perfection of God Himself—it is not the attainment of the ideal, but as close an approach as possible to the ideal. "I am not made perfect already," writes St. Paul; "rather I press on, in the hope that I may iay hold of that for which Christ laid hold of me. I do not count myself to have laid hold of it already; yet one thing I do: I forget what is behind, and strain forward to what is before, and press on towards the goal" (Philip. 3,12,14).

3. The ideal of Christian perfection is fully realized only in the God-Man Jesus Christ.—

Jesus Christ alone was without sin or defect. The holiest of men grieve over their sins and imperfections. Christ, though most humble, was not conscious of sin. He manifested the practice of all virtues in His life in an heroic degree. His charity and filial devotion towards God were most perfect. His charity towards men was profound, universal, efficacious. He loved all—Jews, Samaritans, Gentiles, the children, the poor, the infirm, the afflicted, the just, the sinners. Even Judas is His "friend." His love never degenerated into weakness. To the deepest humility and meekness He united dignity, magnanimity, and the most perfect sincerity. His firmness remained unshaken even in the torture of His passion, wherein He displayed heroic patience, praying for His persecutors and recommending His soul to His Father (GARRIGOU-LAGRANGE).

4. Jesus Christ invited all men to follow Him, to imitate His example.—He calls Himself the Way, the Truth, and the Life. When the rich young man asked Him what he was to do in order to be perfect, the answer was: "Follow Me." "Learn of Me, take up your cross and follow Me" . . . this is His invitation to all seekers after truth and holiness.

"Put ye on the Lord Jesus Christ," is St. Paul's admonition to the Romans (13,14). All the preaching and labor of the great apostle had but one aim: "to present every man perfect in Christ," so that all might "attain to the full knowledge of the Son of God, to the perfect man, to the full measure of the stature of Christ" (Col. 1.28; Eph. 4,13).

5. Therefore the shortest and surest road to perfection is to imitate Jesus Christ in all our actions.—Christ is the model and pattern for every age and condition, for children and adults, for youths and maidens, for rich and poor, for masters and servants. All can imitate Him. "If thou wilt be perfect . . . come . . . follow Me."

In the Eight Beatitudes Christ has left us a summary of His teaching on Christian perfection. They are a declaration of independence from the spirit of the world, which is diametrically opposed to the spirit of Christ. The Christian who practices the doctrine of the Beatitudes is a true follower of Christ and on the road to perfection.

(Read the eight beatitudes in Matt. 5,3-10 carefully. What virtue does each sentence inculcate? How did our Lord practice this virtue? How can you practice it? How is this virtue opposed to the spirit of the world?)

6. There are general and special means to attain perfection.—The general means are at the disposal of all, and all are obliged to make use of them. They may be summed up under four heads:

a) We must love prayer, gladly hear the word of God, assist at Mass devoutly, and often receive the Sacraments. In the Acts of the Apostles we read that the first Christians "were persevering in the doctrine of the Apostles, and in the communication of the breaking of bread, and in prayers" (Acts 2,42);

b) We must constantly deny and mortify ourselves. "If any man will come after Me, let him deny himself and take up his cross daily, and follow Me" (Luke 9,23);

c) We must perform our daily actions in the state of grace, carefully, and with a good intention;

d) We must be patient under trials and afflictions.

5. THE EVANGELICAL COUNSELS

1. The Counsels of Perfection.—Besides these general

"Be ye perfect, as your Heavenly Father is perfect." (Matt. 5, 48)

means, there are also *special means* for attaining perfection, namely, the three *evangelical counsels*: voluntary *poverty*, perpetual *chastity*, and complete *obedience* to a spiritual superior.

They are called *counsels*, because no one is forced to practice them; they are called *evangelical*, because they are recommended in the Gospel (Latin, *Evangelium*).

Christ chose poverty for His bride. "The foxes have holes, and the birds of the air nests; but the Son of Man hath not where to lay His head" (Matt. 8,20). He was born of a Virgin and made the chaste Joseph the guardian of the Christmas mystery. He was obedient to Mary and Joseph; His food was to do the will of His heavenly Father; He became obedient even to the death of the Cross.

Thus we see that those who practice the evangelical counsels follow Christ more closely, imbibe His spirit more deeply, and combat the spirit of the world more effectually. By voluntary poverty they overcome the "concupiscence of the eyes"—the inordinate love and desire of earthly goods; by perpetual chastity their hearts are freed from the bonds of sensuality—the "concupiscence of the flesh"; by obedience to the will of another they apply the best antidote against the poison of false self-love—"the pride of life." The faithful observance of the evangelical counsels not only makes the Christian more Christlike, but also removes the chief obstacles to Christian perfection.

2. These special means of attaining perfection cannot, of their very nature, be binding on all.—After God had created our first parents, He said to them: "Increase and multiply and fill the earth and subdue it." Nor does Holy Scripture make them binding on all. In His conversation with the rich young man Our Lord carefully distinguishes between what is *necessary* for salvation and what is *freely chosen as better and more perfect*: "If thou wilt enter into life, keep the commandments; if thou wilt be perfect, go, sell what thou hast and give to the poor." Of perpetual virginity He says: "All men receive not this word; he that can receive it, let him receive it" (Matt. 19,12). St. Paul makes the same distinction between counsel and precept (1 Cor. 7,32-35).

3. Commandments and Counsels.—According to Scripture and the constant teaching of the Church there is the following difference between a commandment and a counsel:

a) A *commandment* prescribes what is necessary; it binds all men in virtue of the Divine Will; it can be fulfilled by all; its transgression draws down punishment on the offender.

b) A *counsel* recommends what is better and more difficult; it is confined to a limited number; it is binding only on those who have freely resolved to follow it; it brings those who observe it a greater reward in this world and in the next.

4. It may be asked: Is anyone ever *obliged* to follow a mode of life based on the evangelical counsels?

We answer: A person might be bound to choose such a life, if he is morally certain that God has called him to it and that his soul's salvation is endangered if he does not follow the divine call. (The case of the rich young man. Matt. 19,17-24.)

6. The Religious State

1. Who Are Religious?—Those who bind themselves by vow to observe the evangelical counsels in a religious order or congregation approved by the Church are called *religious*.

From this definition it follows that all religious orders of men and women have spiritual perfection for their *end*; the three vows of poverty, chastity and obedience as the *principal means* to that end; rules and constitutions to *regulate their daily lives*; and the approval of the Church as a guarantee that their mode of life is pleasing to God.

2. It is a most praiseworthy thing to enter the religious state, for by doing so a person chooses a state of Christian perfection and is more certain of possessing peace and happiness even in this world and of obtaining special graces for salvation. "Every one that has left home, or brethren, or sisters, or father, or mother, or wife, or children, or lands for My name's sake, shall receive a hundredfold, and shall possess life everlasting" (Matt. 19,29).

3. No one is directly excluded from the religious life who is qualified by natural gifts and wishes to be perfect; in other words, who has a *vocation*.

The mind of the Church on what is called *religious vocation* is expressed by Pope Pius X. He solemnly declared that vocation to the religious life in no way consists, at least as a necessary and ordinary condition, in an *inspiration* given to the subject, that is, in an *invitation by the Holy Ghost*. Nothing else is required, he says, in the aspirants to the religious life than a

"If thou wilt be perfect, go sell what thou hast, and give to the poor and thou shalt have treasure in heaven: and come follow Me." (Matt. 19, 21)

right intention, together with a fitness founded on endowments of nature and grace confirmed by a virtuous life as may afford well-grounded hope that they will rightly discharge their functions and remain faithful to the obligations of their state.

4. The religious state is not only supremely *useful* for those who embrace it; it has also proved most beneficial to the Church by supplying her with excellent workers in every field of Christian endeavor—in spreading the Gospel, in educating the young, in combating error, in reclaiming the fallen, in caring for the orphan, the sick, and the aged. At every epoch of the history of the Church religious orders have contributed largely to the material, intellectual, and artistic progress of society.

"The Christian becomes conscious of keener spiritual impulses, and quickened courage when he recalls to mind the great company of souls who have embraced the religious life, and whom the love of God has inspired to the costliest sacrifices. Who shall reckon up the number of those who have been shamed out of sinful and un-Christlike ways by the thought of the holy lives being lived in cloister and hospital, and who have drawn thence an inspiration to the practice of Christian virtue?" (PESCH, *Christian Philosophy of Life*).

5. In spite of her high esteem for the religious life, the Church has ever held that there is **no twofold ideal of perfection,** one for the religious and one for the Christian in the world: for both the measure of their love of God is the measure of their perfection. *Habitus non facit monachum.*—"The habit does not make the monk." "Habit and tonsure," say Thomas à Kempis, "profit little; but change of heart and perfect mortification of the passions make a true monk." Many men and women in the world have attained as high a degree of sanctity as those who have spent their lives in convents and monasteries. Great saints of God have been found, and are still found, in every state and condition of life.

SUGGESTIONS FOR STUDY AND REVIEW

1. ELEMENTS OF A MORAL ACT

1. When is a human act morally good? When is it morally bad?
2. What is meant by the *object* of an act? If the object is bad, can the act ever be good?
3. Is there such a thing as a *morally indifferent* act? Give examples.
4. What is meant by the *circumstance* of an act? How can circumstances make an act better or worse? Is it worse to rob a bank or a poor box of twenty dollars, and why?
5. What is meant by the *end* of an act? Can the end (intention or motive) make a bad act good? Would you be allowed to tell a lie in order to get a good position for yourself or a friend?
6. Under what conditions is it lawful to perform an action which produces two effects, one good, the other bad?
7. May I dig a well in my property to obtain a supply of water which I need very much, although I know that my well will dry up my neighbor's water-supply? Would the case be different if I were to dig a well in my land to spite my neighbor and to deprive him of his water-supply?
8. Is it true that the Jesuits teach that the end justifies the means? (See Conway, *The Question Box,* p. 434-435).

2. VIRTUE, OR MORAL GOOD AS A HABIT

1. When is a person said to be virtuous?
2. What is virtue? Explain the derivation of the word. Did the pagans look upon humility and meekness as virtues?
3. We speak of *natural* virtues. What do we mean by them?
4. Why are all Christian virtues called *supernatural* virtues? When are they implanted in the soul? What must we do with the seeds of these virtues?
5. What is the difference between the *Theological* and the *Moral* Virtues?

3. THE MORAL VIRTUES

1. Why are some virtues called Moral Virtues?
2. To what four virtues can all the Moral Virtues be reduced? Why are these virtues called Cardinal Virtues?

3. Describe a *prudent* person. We say that St. Aloysius was very prudent. Why?

4. Who is *just*? What other virtues accompany Justice? Why does Holy Scripture call St. Joseph a "just man"?

5. When is a person *temperate*? Quote some proverbs in praise of Temperance. What other virtues are necessary in order to be temperate?

6. Distinguish between *Fortitude* and rashness. Can we be true Christians without possessing the virtue of Fortitude in a high degree? Explain.

7. What virtues are closely allied to Fortitude?

8. Which Moral Virtue is also numbered among the Gifts of the Holy Ghost?

9. Comment on the following saying: "Fortitude without Prudence is but rashness; Prudence without Justice is but craftiness; Justice without Temperance is but cruelty; Temperance without Fortitude is but savageness."

4. CHRISTIAN PERFECTION

1. Who is a perfect Christian?

2. Why can no one in this life attain perfection fully? What does St. Paul say about himself and his striving after perfection?

3. Show how the ideal of Christian perfection was realized in Christ.

4. Which is the surest and shortest road to perfection?

5. Where do we find a summary of Christ's teaching on perfection?

6. Copy the Eight Beatitudes (Matt. 5,3-10). What virtue does each sentence indicate? How did Our Lord practice this virtue? How is this virtue opposed to the spirit of the world?

7. What means must all Christians make use of to attain perfection?

8. *Reading:*

   a) Cardinal Manning, *The Internal Mission of the Holy Ghost,* pp. 321-342: "The Beatitudes."

   b) Tilmann Pesch, S. J., *Christian Philosophy of Life,* pp. 296-298: "Christ the Realization of Humanity's Ideal."

5. THE EVANGELICAL COUNSELS

1. Which are the *special means* of attaining perfection? Why are they called Evangelical Counsels?

2. Show how Christ practiced the counsels which He gave us.

3. Why is the practice of the Evangelical Counsels such an excellent means of attaining perfection?

4. Why are the Evangelical Counsels not binding on all?

5. What is the difference between a commandment and a counsel?

6. Is anyone ever *obliged* to follow a life based on the Evangelical Counsels?

6. THE RELIGIOUS STATE

1. Who is called a *Religious*? Would you be a religious if you bound yourself by vow to observe poverty, chastity, and obedience to a spiritual superior?

2. Why is it a most praiseworthy thing to enter the religious life?
3. Show that the religious state has proved most beneficial to the Church.
4. "The habit does not make the monk." Comment on these words.
5. Write a brief essay on *Vocation to the Religious Life,* using the following outline:

    1) May every boy and girl aspire to be a religious?

    2) If you owed debts, or if your parents were so poor that they needed your help, should you apply for admission into a religious order?

    3) Signs of a Vocation: (*a*) A right intention. In what does this consist? (*b*) Fitness to discharge the duties of a religious life. In what does this fitness consist? (*c*) A virtuous life. (*d*) Are exceptional talents or high education necessary?

    4) If you tried several times to become a religious, but were always rejected by the superiors, would that be a sign that you had no vocation?

    5) It is well for a person to consult his confessor before coming to a final decision on his vocation. (Prayer for light is necessary, but a special illumination or an interior impulse and attraction is not always to be looked for.)

    6) A rejected vocation: Christ and the Rich Young Man (Matt. 19,16-22).

    7) What you may look for in the religious life: *Imitation of Christ,* Bk. I, ch. 17: "Of a Religious Life."

CHAPTER III

Moral Evil

1. NATURE OF SIN

We are created to love God, to do God's will. If we love ourselves more than God, if we do our own will instead of God's will, we commit *sin*.

1. Sin and Guilt, Redemption and Forgiveness of Sin— these are amongst the most important and fundamental truths revealed to us by God. It was Christ's mission to call sinners to repentance (Matt. 9,13). He teaches His disciples to pray for forgiveness of their sins. Whoever humbles himself before God and acknowledges his sins receives forgiveness, whereas pride and hypocrisy make forgiveness impossible (Luke 18,9). Several times we see Him forgiving people's sins, and on one occasion He vindicates His power to forgive sins by a miracle (Mark 2,1-12). He redeemed mankind from sin by His death: "The Son of Man is come to give His life for the redemption of many" (Mark 10,45). He is the Lamb of God that taketh away the sin of the world (John 1,29).

2. Sin is defined by St. Augustine as *factum vel dictum vel concupitum aliquid contra legem aeternam—any thought, word or deed against the eternal law of God.* Sin is the turning away from God, our true end, and the fixing of the affections on something forbidden by the law of God.

That sin is a turning away from our true end, is well brought out by the Greek word for sin, *hamartia,* which means a "missing of the mark, a bad shot."

3. Sin is possible because we possess free will, which we can abuse and turn against the purpose for which God gave it to us.

There is much in our nature which we cannot change, such as our inclinations to pride and sensuality, our proneness to vanity, anger, sloth, obstinacy. All these things, which Scripture calls *concupiscence,* incite us more or less powerfully to sin. But in themselves they are not sinful, for sin is only possible where free will comes into action. "If we look back over our past life, we shall clearly see the difference between *impulses to sin* due to our natural appetites, and certain thoughts, words and deeds which we might have avoided, had we so willed. Hence sin has its roots in the freedom of the will: *it is a willful transgression of what we know to be God's will"* (PESCH, *The Christian Philosophy of Life*).

Schnorr

"And behold they brought to Him one sick of the palsy. . . . And Jesus, seeing their faith, said to the man sick of the palsy: 'Be of good heart, son, thy sins are forgiven thee.'" (Matt. 9, 2)

4. In the light of reason sin is hateful,

a) Because it humiliates and degrades our nature; hence comes the sense of shame which a person experiences when detected in a lie, a theft, or some other wicked deed;

b) Because it is often an injury to our fellow-men, always an injury to ourselves; .

c) Because in itself and in its effects it is a disturbance of the moral order of which God is the source.

5. In the light of faith sin is hateful and the greatest of all evils, because, in its inmost nature, it is—

a) A *rebellion* against God's most holy will, the only true measure of our actions;

b) A *contemptuous defiance* of the almighty Creator;

c) An *insult* offered to the thrice holy God, robbing Him of the honor which is His due;

d) A *base act of ingratitude* towards One so evidently good in Himself, so infinitely good to all men;

e) A *mockery* of Christ and an attempt to crucify Him again (Heb. 6,6);

f) An *assault on our own soul,* on our temporal and eternal happiness: "They that commit sin and iniquity are enemies to their own soul" (Tob. 12,10);

g) A *surrender of true interior liberty and peace:* "Whosoever committeth sin, is the slave of sin" (John 8,34).

2. KINDS OF SIN

1. The word sin is used for three different things:

a) *Original Sin:* a state of complete separation from God inherited from our first parents;

b) *Mortal Sin:* complete separation from God brought about by an act of our own free will;

c) *Venial Sin:* not a complete separation from God, yet a willful deviation from the right path and a weakening of the life of grace.

Mortal and venial sin imply an act of our own free will; original sin does not. Hence according to its *origin* sin is divided into *original* and *actual* sin. According to its *effects* sin is divided into *mortal* and *venial* sin.

2. The distinction between mortal and venial sin is clearly taught in Scripture and has been defined by the Church as an article of faith.

Holy Scripture speaks of sins which deserve death and exclude from the Kingdom of Heaven, and also of less serious transgressions which not even the just can avoid entirely (Rom. 1,32; John 5,16; James 3,2; 1 John 1,8)*.

In accordance with these plain statements of Scripture the Council of Trent declared against the Protestant reformers, who looked upon all sins alike as mortal, that "no one, not even the most holy, can avoid sin altogether, except by a special privilege of God, as the Church holds concerning the Blessed Virgin." Hence it follows

* Yet God will give the grace necessary to avoid any sin, so that no one can say he could not help committing a sin. God "will not suffer you to be tempted above that which you are able..." (1 Cor. 10:13). —*Editor,* 1990.

that some sins are mortal, others venial; that some sins destroy holiness, others not.

Our reason also tells us that there must be a distinction between mortal and venial sins. "There is an analogy between human friendship and the friendship of the soul with God. Just as some offenses are sufficient to destroy friendship entirely, while others only weaken it, so there are some sins which destroy, others which only weaken the love of God in the soul." There is a *malice* of the will, and what proceeds from it is mortal sin; and there is a *weakness* of the will, and what proceeds from it is venial sin,* of which we can say: "to err is human." "Venial sin," says St. Thomas, "is a *disease* of the soul, not its *death*, and grace is still left by which it may be repaired. Mortal sin is irreparable, and a person who is guilty of it has lost every principle of vitality; he is as unable to recover life as one who has suffered bodily death. Renewal cannot come from within, but only from the almighty power of God, Who can make even the dead hear His Voice and live."

The difference between mortal and venial sin is so *essential* that any number of venial sins cannot make a mortal sin. Still we must never forget that every venial sin is a step towards mortal sin, and that punishment follows on it either here or in the world to come. "He that contemneth small things shall fall little by little" (Ecclus. 19,1).

3. Since mortal sin is the greatest of all evils, it is important to know **what makes a real mortal sin.** There must be three conditions present:

a) The thing done must be very bad—*grave matter.*

b) It must be done with full knowledge of its sinfulness—*advertence.*

c) And with full consent of the will—*deliberation.*

The absence of any one of these conditions will make a sin not mortal, or not a sin at all. (Illustrate by suitable examples.)

4. It is not easy to decide in each particular case what is or is not mortal sin. We know we cannot fall away from God without a deliberate act of the will; hence, if we want to walk securely on the path of duty, we must strive to avoid every *deliberate* transgression of the law of God.

*It is of course true that one can also commit a mortal sin out of *weakness*; a sin need not be committed out of *malice* in order to be mortal. —Editor, 1990.

Some sins, such as blasphemy, apostasy, perjury, impurity, murder, are, if deliberate, always mortal; others, like theft, though mortal in their own nature, are venial if the amount of wrong done is small; others again, such as lying, are venial in their own nature, and only become mortal under certain circumstances. (Recall what was said above about the circumstances of our acts.)

5. Mortal sins differ very much in gravity. Thus sins whose direct object is God, such as blasphemy or apostasy, are greater than sins of impurity or theft, whose direct objects are ourselves or our fellow-men.

Venial sins are usually divided into *deliberate* and *indeliberate*. By indeliberate is meant "With imperfect deliberation," because there cannot be such a thing as a really indeliberate sin.

3. TEMPTATION AND THE OCCASIONS OF SIN

By the world outside us, by our own human nature, and by the devil through both, we are frequently incited to act against the will of God. What St. Paul says of himself is true of all of us: "I delight in the law of God after the inward man, but I behold another law in my members, fighting against the law of my mind, and making me captive to the law of sin" (Rom. 7,22).

1. What is Temptation?—*This incitement to choose some personal satisfaction in place of the will of God is called temptation.* "So long as we live in this world," says Thomas à Kempis, "we cannot be without tribulation and temptation. Hence it is written in Job: The life of man upon earth is a life of temptation. No man is so perfect and holy but he hath sometimes temptation."

2. In every temptation we can distinguish three steps: the occasion of the temptation, the temptation itself, and the outcome or issue.

a) The *occasion* of a temptation is either some external object that falls under our senses or some stimulus, feeling or emotion within us. By these the corresponding passions or desires are aroused. Since the desires cannot be satisfied without violating our moral duties, a conflict arises in our soul between passion and duty.

b) It is precisely this *conflict* that we call *temptation*. Our own evil passions are, therefore, the real source of every temptation. "Let no man, when he is tempted, say that he is tempted by God. For God is not a tempter of evils, and He tempteth no man. But every man is tempted by his own concupiscence, being drawn away and allured" (James 1,13).

c) The temptation *comes to an end* at the moment when our will decides either for or against what we know to be our duty. Sometimes no decision is reached. The conflict continues for a time, and then dies out, either because the evil desire vanishes from our consciousness, or because our attention is interrupted and directed into other channels (F. TILLMANN).

3. Temptation Is Not Sin.—From what has been said it follows that temptation is a *conflict* but *no sin*, not even an imperfection. Many are disquieted by the evil thoughts and suggestions which flash into their minds; they must remember that *where the will withholds consent there is no sin.* No matter how strong the temptation may be, or how long it may last, provided only our will remains true, there can be no question of sin.

4. Temptations Useful.—Temptations are a great trial and burden, but we must not forget that God would not permit them unless they were *useful* in many ways. The Holy Ghost promises the victor's crown to all who have stood the test of temptation: "Blessed is the man that endureth temptation, for when he hath been proved, he shall receive the crown of life, which God hath promised to them that love Him" (James 1,12).

Temptation steels and fortifies the will. "The greater the force of the wind, the deeper the tree seeks to strike root into the soil."

In temptation we become aware of our helplessness and learn to cast ourselves with humility and childlike trust into the arms of God.

When there is conflict, a great saint has said, there is courage, vigilance, fidelity, wisdom, prudence, firmness, ardor, endurance,

5. Prepare to Meet Temptation.—If temptations are to be useful to us, we must be *prepared to meet them* in the right way.

a) Prayer is the all-important means for gaining the victory in temptations. "Watch and pray that you enter not into temptation," was Our Lord's injunction to His disciples. And St. Peter says: "Be you humbled under the mighty hand of God, that He might exalt you in the time of visitation, casting all your care upon Him, for He hath care of you" (1 Pet. 5,6).

b) In times of peace we must prepare for war, training our will by deliberate acts of self-denial and self-conquest.

c) We must turn our minds away from the objects and imaginations which, as we know from experience, give rise to temptation.

Overbeck

"And He cometh and findeth them sleeping. And He saith to Peter: 'Simon, sleepest thou? Couldst thou not watch one hour? Watch ye and pray that you enter not into temptation. The spirit indeed is willing, but the flesh is weak.'" (Mark 14, 37-38)

d) We must resist temptation from the very beginning. "The enemy is more easily overcome, if he be not suffered to enter the door of our hearts, but be resisted at the very gate on his first knocking" (*Imitation of Christ*, I, 13,5). Ovid has well said:

> Principiis obsta, sero medicina paratur,
> Dum mala per longas invaluere moras.

> Resist beginnings; all too late the cure,
> When ills have gathered strength through long delay.

e) "Many waters cannot quench charity, neither can the floods drown it" (Cant. 8,7). A real personal love of Christ is the best armor against all the assaults of temptation, whether they come from within or from without, from the world, the devil, or the flesh. In reply to an infamous person who sought to lead her into sin, St. Agatha, the virgin martyr, said: "My mind is firmly settled and grounded in Christ. Your words are winds, your promises are rains, your terrors are floods. With what violence soever they may beat against my house, it can never fail, for it is founded upon solid rock."

6. We cannot avoid temptation, but we are strictly bound to avoid the *proximate occasions of sin*, whenever it is possible.

An occasion of sin is something which commonly leads to sin. There are many such occasions in the world: the reading of a book, a paragraph in a newspaper, a place of amusement, a visit paid or received, a present given or taken, a conversation, a phrase, a word, or even a glance. It is impossible to enumerate them all. They are different for different persons, and different in different circumstances. When we cannot avoid them we must make use of the proper means, natural and supernatural, to counteract their evil influence. "He who loveth danger shall perish therein."

4. SIN AND PUNISHMENT

1. Being wisdom itself, God must have provided a perfect sanction for His law. To suppose otherwise would imply that He could be indifferent to its being observed. His justice, too, demands such a sanction. "For it would be clearly a negation of justice for Him to show Himself equally kind to those who do His will and to those who maliciously set it aside."

2. The eternal God has provided an eternal sanction for the Moral Law.—If we deliberately violate that law in an important matter, we separate ourselves completely from God—we say to His face: *Non serviam*—"I will not serve Thee." And if we die in mortal sin, our separation from God becomes eternal, that is, we are in Hell. We have forfeited our right to the kingdom of light and joy, and our lot is cast with those who dwell in the realm of darkness and eternal pain. Over the gate of hell these dreadful words are written:

> Through me you pass into the city of woe:
> Through me you pass into eternal pain.
> Through me among the people lost for aye.
> All hope abandon, ye who enter here.
> —DANTE, *Inferno*.

In the light of this truth, too plainly written on the pages of the Inspired Word to be doubted or explained away, we catch a glimpse of the abyss of malice and perversity that underlies one single mortal sin; we understand why the Church and all her faithful children wage such fierce and relentless war against sin; we understand why the Saints of God were so passionately afraid of sin.

3. Love and Fear.—Although the noblest motive which ought to inspire us in the battle with sin is *love of God*, still many saints have declared that *fear of God*, of judgment and Hell, was needed to ensure their perseverance in good. They were but doing what Christ bade them do: "Fear Him that can destroy both soul and body into Hell" (Matt. 10,28).

4. If sin is such a dreadful evil, the greatest of all evils, why did God permit it? Why does He not hinder it?—

In every age Christian saints and sages have asked themselves this same question and all have had to admit that sin in its nature and in its consequences is the *mysterium iniquitatis*, the mystery of iniquity (2 Thess. 2,7), which remains insoluble to our earthly knowledge.

One thing is certain: Divine Wisdom has good grounds for not hindering the entrance of sin into this world. We do not see those grounds now, or at most only "in a dark manner," but we have no right on that account to question them. God has revealed Himself to us as infinitely lovable, kind, and merciful, and it is our duty to love Him in return. But *confidence* in the beloved is essential to love. "The old pagan legend of *Eros and Psyche* is a beautiful illustration of this truth. Psyche's sufferings are all the result of an impatient and self-willed desire to know all about her husband. Those who truly love must have such faith in the goodness and in the love of the beloved that they are content to remain in ignorance, if he so will, since they are certain that the action they can not understand is noble and right. Even such a confidence does our Lord ask of souls who would love Him. 'What I do thou knowest not now, but thou shalt know hereafter.' If we have, as we have indeed, all reason to trust and love the Divine Speaker of these words, we ought surely to rest in content with the difficulties appointed in this life *to give our faith its trial, its perfection and its merit*."—E. I. WATKIN, *Some Thoughts on Catholic Apologetics* (St. Louis: B. Herder Book Co.), p. 49.

SUGGESTIONS FOR STUDY AND REVIEW

1. NATURE OF SIN.   2. KINDS OF SIN

1. How does St. Augustine define sin? Why do we say that sin is "a turning away from God"?
2. Why is sin possible?
3. Show the hatefulness of sin: (*a*) in the light of reason; (*b*) in the light of faith.
4. How many kinds of sin are there?
5. Show from Scripture and reason that a clear-cut distinction must be made between Mortal and Venial Sin. Illustrate your answer by examples.
6. What makes a real mortal sin? Give examples.

3. Temptation and the Occasions of Sin

1. What is Temptation? Whence do temptations mainly come?
2. What three steps can we distinguish in every temptation?
3. Is temptation a sin? Explain.
4. Show that temptations can be very useful to us.
5. How must we prepare to meet temptations?
6. What is meant by the proximate occasions of sin?
7. What must we do if we cannot avoid the proximate occasions of sin?
8. Read the account of Christ's temptation in Matt. 4,1-11. To what kind of temptations did Our Lord permit Himself to be subjected? How did He overcome each? Why did He allow the devil to tempt Him? Could Christ be tempted from within as we are often tempted?
9. You have to deal with disagreeable and uncongenial companions. What will you, as a rule, be tempted to do? What should you do?
10. You dislike certain persons. You are inclined to be jealous or envious of them. Or you think them proud and overbearing. You feel a strong inclination to say harsh things about them or to exaggerate their faults. How are you going to deal with these inclinations? Can you do more than merely resist them?
11. *Reading:*
    a) *Imitation of Christ,* Bk. I, ch. 13: "Of Resisting Temptation."
    b) *Question Box,* pp. 277-278: "The Occasions of Sin."
    c) James 4,2; 1 Cor. 10,13; Phil. 4,13. What do these texts show?

4. Sin and Punishment

1. Why must God have provided a *sanction,* (i.e., penalties for the transgression and rewards for the observance) for His Law?
2. What punishment is due to mortal sin? To venial sin?
3. Which is the noblest motive that should inspire us in our battle with sin? Is the motive of fear a good motive?
4. "If mortal sin is such a dreadful evil, the greatest of all evils, why did God permit it? Why does He not hinder it?" What answer would you give to these questions?
5. *A Lesson to be learned:* Avoid mortal sin as the one great evil. "Flee from sins as from the face of a serpent" (Ecclus. 21,2). Avoid all such occasions as may lead to it. Seek in prayer and the Sacraments strength to resist it. If in sin, make an act of perfect contrition, and hasten to confession. "None see the nature of sin so clearly as those who are freest from it."

SECTION II

SPECIAL MORAL

Introduction

It is the aim of *Special Moral* to apply the general principles of Christian Morality to man as an individual and as a member of society. As an individual man has duties to God and to himself, as a member of the great human family he has duties to his fellow-men, and special duties as a member of his own little family, of the State, and the Church.

All these duties are summarized in the *Two Great Commandments of Love*: "Thou shalt love the Lord thy God with thy whole heart, and with thy whole soul and with thy whole mind. This is the greatest and the first commandment. And the second is like to this: Thou shalt love thy neighbor as thyself" (Matt. 22,36-39).

These two commandments are the greatest, because they practically contain all the others. The one aim of the Ten Commandments, or the *Decalogue* (Greek, *ten words*) is to help us to carry out the great commandment of love: "He that hath My Commandments and keepeth them, he it is that loveth Me" (John 14,21). The first three of the Ten Commandments refer to the love of God; the last seven to the love of ourselves and of our neighbor.

These three spheres of duty form the subject matter of Special Moral. In other words, Special Moral answers the following questions:

1. What are our duties to God?
2. What are our duties to ourselves?
3. What are our duties to our fellow-men?
4. What are our duties to our fellow-men as members of the family, the State, and the Church?

Since all duty springs from law, and all law comes from God, all duties are duties to God.

SUGGESTIONS FOR STUDY AND REVIEW

1. What is the aim of Special Moral?
2. What duties have we as individuals? As members of society?
3. In what two commandments are all our duties summed up?
4. What questions does Special Moral answer?
5. *Reading:* Exodus 19,10-19 and 20,1-20.

THE SOLEMN PROMULGATION OF THE DECALOGUE

And the Lord spoke all these words:

"I am the Lord thy God, who brought thee out of the land of Egypt, out of the house of bondage.

"Thou shalt not have strange gods before Me.

"Thou shalt not make to thyself a graven thing, nor the likeness of any thing that is in heaven above, or in the earth beneath, nor of those things that are in the waters under the earth.

"Thou shalt not adore them, nor serve them: I am the Lord thy God, mighty, jealous, visiting the iniquity of the fathers upon the children, unto the third and fourth generation of them that hate Me:

"And showing mercy unto thousands of them that love Me and keep My commandments.

"Thou shalt not take the name of the Lord thy God in vain: for the Lord will not hold him guiltless that shall take the name of the Lord his God in vain.

"Remember thou keep holy the Sabbath Day.

"Six days shalt thou labor, and shalt do all thy works, but on the seventh day is the Sabbath of the Lord thy God: thou shalt do no work on it, thou, nor thy son, nor thy daughter, nor thy man-servant, nor thy maid-servant, nor thy beast, nor the stranger that is within thy gates.

"For in six days the Lord made heaven and earth, and the sea, and all things that are in them, and rested on the seventh day, and sanctified it.

"Honor thy father and thy mother, that thou mayest be long-lived upon the land which the Lord thy God will give thee.

"Thou shalt not kill.

"Thou shalt not commit adultery.

"Thou shalt not steal.

"Thou shalt not bear false witness against thy neighbor.

"Thou shalt not covet thy neighbor's house: neither shalt thou desire his wife, nor his servant, nor his hand-maid. nor his ox, nor his ass, nor anything that is his."

And all the people saw the voices and the flames, and the sound of the trumpet, and the mount smoking: and, being terrified and struck with fear, they stood afar off, saying to Moses:

"Speak thou to us, and we will hear; let not the Lord speak to us, lest we die."

And Moses said to the people: "Fear not, for God is come to prove you, and that the dread of Him might be in you, and you should not sin."

Fugel

THE PROMULGATION OF THE DECALOGUE

CHAPTER I

Our Duties to God

God being our First Cause and our Last End, we must surrender ourselves completely to Him, if we wish to attain the purpose of our existence. This surrender of ourselves is accomplished by the practice of the three Theological Virtues of Faith, Hope, and Charity. *Faith* reveals God's truth to us; *Hope* points to the possession of God as our life's goal; *Charity* unites us with God. The fruit of our self-surrender to God is the virtue of *Religion*. Hence we shall first treat of the Theological Virtues, and then of the virtue of Religion.

A. The Three Theological Virtues

1. Faith

a) NATURE, PROPERTIES, AND DUTIES OF FAITH

1. Catholic Faith is a virtue infused by the Holy Ghost into our souls at Baptism, by which we believe, firmly and without hesitation, all that God has revealed and through the Church proposes for our belief. The truths of faith are contained in Holy Scripture and Tradition. They are confided to the keeping of the Church, who makes them known to the faithful through her ministers.

Raphael

FAITH

53

2. We must carefully distinguish Faith from *knowledge* gained by experience or in any other way. **Faith rests entirely on the authority of another;** Christian Faith, on the *authority of God.* What makes our Faith *divine* is believing the truths of revelation because God, who is Truth itself, and Who cannot deceive us, has revealed them to us. What He has revealed must be true, whether we understand it or not.

3. Catholic Faith is living Faith, that is, it must be at the root of our whole religious life. Only that is true faith, says St. Gregory the Great, which does not contradict in works what is believed in words. Faith without works that spring from it is dead. "If I should have all faith, so that I could remove mountains, and have not charity, I am nothing" (1 Cor. 13,2).

4. Catholic Faith embraces all revelation.—God vouches for the truth of all revelation, and therefore also for every single revealed truth. Hence Catholic Faith is also a *firm* and *unwavering* faith; for it is founded on God and is a work of His grace. Faith and doubt are incompatible.

5. Catholic Faith is a conquering and unconquerable Faith.—It is ready to make any sacrifice, even that of life itself. "This is the victory which overcometh the world, our faith" (1 John 5,4).

"At the time of the great Irish famine (1845-1847) many depots were opened by proselytising societies for distributing food to the starving people, gratis indeed, but at the price of giving up the Catholic faith and being instructed or numbered as Protestants. Then a cerain widow in northwest Kerry, seeing her children wasting away with hunger, herself unable to save them, and across the way one of these depots filled with food, in her bewilderment and without evil intent asked the eldest boy, who was but ten years old, to cross over and simply show himself at the depot in the hope that the very sight of his wretchedness would move the distributors to minister to his hunger without assailing his faith. But then as promptly as if he had been Lewis of Japan or Dorotheus of Rome, the boy answered, 'Ah, mother, death were better.' So with his two brothers this child of faith and fortitude died slowly of starvation."—DEVAS, *The Key to the World's Progress* (New York: Longmans, Green & Co.).

6. The Pearl of Great Price.—Since without Faith it is impossible to please God (Heb. 11,6), Faith is *God's choicest gift to man and man's most valuable possession.* It is the "pearl of great price, which when the merchant had found, he went his way, and sold all that he had, and bought it" (Matt. 13,46). Hence we are in duty bound—

a) To keep our faith alive and active—to "live by faith," as the Apostle says;

b) To profess our Faith openly and without fear of the consequences, whenever God's honor, or the salvation of our neighbor, or the cause of religion demands it;

c) To shun all that is likely to endanger our Faith;

d) To broaden and deepen our knowledge of the truths of faith;

e) To make frequent acts of faith; such prayerful consideration of the divine grounds of our faith cannot but strengthen our faith and help us to overcome doubts and difficulties that assail it.

b) SINS AGAINST FAITH

The sins which are essentially opposed to Faith may be classed under five headings: *Infidelity, Heresy, Apostasy, Skepticism* or *Doubt*, and *Indifferentism*.

a) Those who do not believe in the doctrines of Christ are said to be in a state of **Infidelity.** When Infidelity arises from involuntary or invincible ignorance of the Christian teachings, it is not a sin. "If I had not come and spoken to them, they would not have sin, but now they have no excuse for their sins" (John 15,22). But if a person is perfectly convinced of the truth of the Christian Religion and yet refuses to embrace it, he is without excuse: "He that believeth not, shall be condemned" (Mark 16,16).

Under *Infidelity* we rank *Paganism, Judaism,* and *Mohammedanism.* We call all those pagans who are either in reality or professedly without faith, such as *Atheists,* who deny the existence of God; *Deists,* who believe in the existence of God, but deny His Providence and reject all revelation; and *Idolaters* (Greek, *Eidolon,* an image), who pay divine honors to false gods.

b) A Christian who denies a single truth of faith or defends a doctrine opposed to any article of faith, commits the sin of **Heresy** (Greek, *hairesis,* choice). Heresy may be defined as "the obstinate adherence of a baptized Christian to some error directly opposed to any article of faith, that is, to a truth which the Church proposes for our belief, as being revealed by God."

If a Christian were unconsciously to hold an error, he would be what is called a *material heretic;* if he were conscious of his error, and still persisted in it, he would be a *formal heretic.* Formal heresy incurs the penalty of excommunication.

Schism (Greek, *schisma,* a tear or rent) is a revolt against the authority of the Church, a formal separation from the unity of the Church. In itself it is not a sin against faith, but a grave sin of disobedience. In most cases, however, it is joined with heresy, because the schismatic, as a rule, also denies the supreme ruling and teaching power of the Sovereign Pontiff, which is an article of faith.

c) **Apostasy** is the entire abandonment of the Christian Faith by one who has been baptized. It is a more grievous sin than refusal to accept the Christian religion, because it implies at the same time a revolt against Christ and His Church.

Apostasy differs from *Denial of the Faith.* He who denies the faith by words, signs, or deeds, still clings to it in his heart, but lacks the courage to profess it when bound to do so. Grave causes may at times arise which justify, not a *denial* of our faith, but a concealment of it from others. The mere fact of not undeceiving people who mistake us for non-Catholics does not constitute a denial of our faith, provided we use no improper means to conceal it.

"Apostasy is of all misfortunes the worst that can befall men. There may be excuses, mitigating circumstances, for our greatest sins, but here it is useless to seek for any. God gives faith. It is lost only through our own fault. God abandons them who abandon Him. Apostasy is the most patent case of spiritual suicide, and the apostate carries branded on his forehead the mark of reprobation. A miracle can save him, but nothing short of a miracle can do it, and who has a right to expect it? God is good, but God is also just" (Stapleton).

d) **Doubts** concerning any article of the faith should at once be banished from our minds; for if they are voluntary and deliberately consented to, they are grave sins. Willfully to doubt what God has revealed, is to call in question the Divine truthfulness, is really formal heresy, or if it embraces the fundamental truths of faith, apostasy.

We must distinguish doubts from difficulties.—The supposed conflict between Faith and Science is a fruitful source of difficulties which try the faith of so many Catholics in our day. We have the right and the duty to look these difficulties square in the face and to seek an answer to them. Even if we do not immediately find the proper solution, we know that there is one, because true science cannot contradict the infallible word of God. God is the author of nature and its laws as well as of revelation.

Like other temptations, temptations against the faith are not without great profit to us. Difficulties earnestly met and overcome intensify and strengthen our faith. A faith that we have fought hard for is no longer merely something, however precious, that has been handed on to us by our parents—we have made it our very own; and our faith, which alone gives a meaning and a value to our life, is surely something worth fighting for.

"Many persons," says Cardinal Newman, "are very sensitive of the difficulties of Religion; I am as sensitive of them as any one; but I have never been able to see a connection between apprehending those difficulties, however keenly, and multiplying them to any extent, and on the other hand doubting the doctrines to which they are attached. *Ten thousand difficulties do not make one doubt,* as I understand the subject; difficulty and doubt are incommensurate. There of course may be difficulties in the evidence; but I am speaking of difficulties intrinsic to the doctrines themselves, or to their relations with each other. A man may be annoyed that he cannot work out a mathematical problem, of which the answer is or is not given to him, without doubting that it admits of an answer, or that a certain particular answer is the true one. Of all points of faith, the being of a God is, to my own apprehension, encompassed with most difficulty, and yet borne in upon our minds with most power" (*Apologia pro Vita Sua,* p. 239).

e) **Indifferentism** in matters of faith can be *theoretical* or *practical.* Theoretical indifferentism maintains that it is of no consequence what religion a man may follow, either because all are false or because none can be proved to be true. Such indifferentism is apostasy in one who once professed the Christian religion, and therefore a very grave sin. That sort of indifferentism which, without renouncing the Christian religion, holds it to be a matter of indifference to what denomination one may belong, is a species of heresy. It denies at least one clearly defined article of the faith, viz., that the Catholic Church is the only true Church.

Practical indifferentism means a growing cold in the practice of faith, a neglect of the duties of faith. It is fostered by mixed marriages and by the reading of secular, that is, religiously indifferent if not positively anti-religious books, magazines and newspapers. It is the religious disease of our day.

c) DANGERS TO THE FAITH

Since Faith is absolutely necessary for salvation, we are bound to ward off, to the best of our ability, every danger that threatens our faith. The Church also, as the guardian of the deposit of faith, has the duty to safeguard her children from loss of the faith. Hence the Church has the right to make laws in this matter, and every Catholic has the duty to obey these laws.

1. The law of the Church forbids Catholics to assist actively at, or take part in, the religious services of non-Catholics.—A *passive* or merely material presence may be tolerated for reasons of civil duty or honor, at funerals, weddings, and similar celebrations, provided no danger of perversion or scandal arises. To attend non-Catholic ceremonies out of mere curiosity, without danger to our faith or scandal to others, might be innocent enough, but is nevertheless to be discouraged.

2. Secret Societies.—Catholics are forbidden to join any society, no matter what its name, if it has the following marks:

a) *Absolute secrecy*; which means keeping acts and proceedings secret from those who have a right to know them.

b) *Blind and unrestricted obedience to leaders.*

c) *Opposition to God's Church or to lawfully established civil government.*

d) *A self-constituted religious worship.*

Freemasonry and all the secret societies allied to it have all these marks and are therefore forbidden by the Church. Those who list their names on the rolls of these societies incur the penalty of excommunication.*

3. The Index.—Faith is often destroyed by the reading of books hostile to the faith or to good morals. The reading of anti-Catholic books by those who have neither the education nor the need to do so, is obviously to run headlong into danger. To obviate this danger the Church has instituted the *Index* (*Index librorum prohibitorum*—list of forbidden books). Those who do possess the requisite learning, and have also a reason, other than mere curiosity, can obtain from the proper authority a dispensation to read condemned books.**

---

*See Can. 1374 of the 1983 Code of Canon Law. —*Editor,* 1990.

**The *Index of Forbidden Books* has been abolished, but the principle remains: It is a sin to read or watch anything that presents a danger to one's Catholic faith or morals. —*Editor,* 1990.

The Acts of the Apostles relates that the converts from paganism at Ephesus brought together their books on magic and burnt them publicly (19,19). Since then Councils and Synods have time and again condemned anti-Catholic books. The Council of Trent established the Congregation of the Index, whose functions are now exercised by the Holy Office.* The Council also ordered the publication of a list of forbidden books. The first *Index* was published in 1564. The laws of the Church in regard to books and reading may be summed up as follows:

a) Translations of the Bible must be approved either by the Holy See or by a Bishop; a Bishop cannot approve them unless they are furnished with explanatory notes.

b) Forbidden are all writings which attack the foundations of religion (the existence of God, the immortality of the soul) or any article of the faith.

c) Forbidden are all writings with an immoral purpose.

Any one who reads such books without permission from his ecclesiastical superiors incurs the penalty of excommunication. The penalty, however, is not incurred by any one who reads such a book without knowing that it was forbidden. **

2. Hope

1. All hope consists of two elements.—(*a*) the *desire* for some valuable good, and (*b*) *confidence* that the desired good will be attained. The *Theological Virtue of Hope* includes both these elements, but points to God as the desired Good and as the basis of our confidence.

Hope is the supernatural gift of God by which we trust that God will give us, through the merits of Jesus Christ, eternal life and all the help necessary to obtain it.

Not only graces, but also temporal goods, such as health and prosperity, are objects of Hope, in so far as they may help us in the way of salvation. "Seek ye first the kingdom of God and His

Raphael

HOPE

*The Holy Office is now called the Sacred Congregation for the Doctrine of the Faith. The *Index* has been abolished. —*Editor*, 1990.

**The penalty of excommunication no longer attaches to the reading of such books, but it remains a sin and may well constitute mortal sin. —*Editor*, 1990.

justice, and all these things shall be added unto you" (Matt. 6,33).

Like Faith, Hope is infused into our souls at Baptism, and like Faith, it is absolutely necessary for salvation. What we know by Faith becomes by Hope the object of all our aspirations and all our striving. Hope directs us to view and to judge all things in the light of our last end—*sub specie aeternitatis.*

Whilst the infidel, according to St. Paul, has no hope (1 Thess. 4,13), the Christian knows that he has not here a lasting city but seeks one that is to come (Heb. 13,14); he directs his mind to the things that are above, where Christ is sitting at the right hand of God (Col. 3,1), and is saved by Hope (Rom. 8,24).

2. Our Hope must have three qualities:

a) It must be a *living* hope, because its purpose is to influence our whole life, to urge us on to the attainment of our eternal destiny with all the powers of our mind and heart.

b) It must be *firm and unwavering.* Only perfect trust in God can give us the high courage necessary to work out our salvation in the face of obstacles that at times seem insurmountable. With Hope cheering him on, the Christian tastes the joy of victory even before the conflict is over (Rom. 12,12).

c) It must be accompanied by *a holy fear and a wholesome distrust* of ourselves. "He that thinketh himself to stand, let him take heed lest he fall" (1 Cor. 10,12). It was by acknowledging his own sinfulness and hoping in Jesus at the last moment that the Good Thief gained paradise.

3. The sins directly opposed to Hope are Despair and Presumption.—

a) We sin by *Despair* whenever we give up hope of arriving at eternal happiness; whenever we regard our sins either as too great or too numerous for pardon, or our passions as too strong to be overcome.

In a lesser degree we sin against Hope when, by want of confidence in the goodness of God, we give up hope of obtaining what we ask for in prayer, because it is deferred.

Despair is a most pernicious evil. It deadens all our spiritual endeavors, fills the soul with sadness, causes us to abandon prayer, and leaves us exposed to every vice.

The surest remedies against Despair are: Prayer, acts of Hope, consideration of the merits of Christ, the goodness, power, and promises of God, His care for all creatures, and His readiness to pardon even the greatest sinners. (Do you know any instances in the New Testament?)

b) We sin by *Presumption,* if we continue to sin with the intention of repenting before death comes; or if we make our salvation depend upon our own strength alone and not upon God; or if we rashly expose ourselves to the proximate occasions of sin in the expectation that God will come to our rescue.

Prayer and humility are the best antidotes against Presumption. We should often think of what the Saints have done to gain heaven, and ever bear in mind the words of Christ: "The kingdom of Heaven suffereth violence, and the violent bear it away" (Matt. 11,12).

True confidence in God requires, therefore, that we should not be *excessively uneasy* about our salvation; and that we should *not throw off all fear and anxiety* in regard to it.

4. Although Hope, like Faith, is a gift of God, still we are bound to nourish it carefully.—In the Epistle to the Hebrews St. Paul again and again urges the Christians to practice this beautiful virtue. "Let us hold fast to the confessions of our hope without wavering, for He is faithful that hath promised" (10,13). He calls Hope "an anchor of the soul, sure and firm" (6,18). Christ is the great High Priest of the good things to come, and only those are made partakers of Him, who hold firm to Him unto the end (9,11).

3. Charity, or Love of God

1. Nature of Charity.—*Charity* is a virtue, or supernatural habit, infused by God into our souls, by which we love God above all things for His own sake and all things for God's sake.

The *object* of Charity is God and all the creatures of God— God for His own sake, and the things created by God for God's sake.

The *motive* of Charity is not one or the other attribute of God, but the *infinite perfection* of God.

Charity may be *perfect* or *imperfect* according to the motive from which our love proceeds. Perfect charity consists in loving God for His own sake. Imperfect charity is an *interested* love:

Raphael

CHARITY
Without charity, though we speak with the tongues of
men and of Angels, we are but "sounding brass and a
tinkling cymbal" (1 Cor. 13,1).

we love God for what He has done for us, or for what we expect
Him to do for us.

Charity is not a mere matter of feeling, not a tender emotion,
which we commonly call love, but it is a *love of preference*. It
resides in the will, which deliberately prefers God before all
things, and is ready to sacrifice all rather than offend Him mortally.

2. Charity Is the Mother and Queen of Virtues.—Christ
called charity the greatest commandment in the Law. St. Paul sings
the glorious canticle of Charity and assigns to it the first place
among the divine virtues (1 Cor. 13). He calls charity the bond
of perfection (Col. 3,14) and the fulfilling of the Law (Rom.
13,10). Even Faith itself is of no value unless "it worketh by
charity" (Gal. 5,6). Without charity, though we speak with the
tongues of men and of Angels, we are but "sounding brass and a
tinkling cymbal" (1 Cor. 13,1).

The reason for this pre-eminence of charity is clear: Whatever
else we may offer to God, whether sacrifice, or prayers, or vows,
all that is not ourselves; it is only by love that we give Him ourselves, our inmost being, the core and kernel of our personality.
"My son, give Me thy heart."

**3. God Himself has told us what qualities our love of Him
should have:**

Mark 12,20: "Thou shalt love the Lord thy God with thy whole
heart, and with thy whole soul, and with thy whole mind, and
with all thy strength"—our charity must be *sovereign*.

John 14,21 : "He that hath My commands and keepeth them, he it is that loveth Me"—our charity must be *active*.

John 13,1 : "Having loved His own who were in the world, He loved them unto the end"—our charity must be generous and *constant*, as is God's love for us.

4. Charity is increased and perfected in us

a) By meditating on the Divine Perfections and on the life and passion of Christ;

b) By making frequent acts of charity and perfect contrition;

c) By fidelity to every duty;

d) By referring our every thought, word, and action to God.

It was at the feet of the Crucifix that a St. Francis of Assisi, a St. Philip Neri, a St. Theresa, and a St. Alphonsus Liguori nourished and ever enkindled anew their love of God. Apart from the very beauty of posture, says a spiritual writer, which makes the crucifix a noble theme of art, there is an exhaustless wealth of beauty which we read into it in the light of faith. *Omnis enim figura eius amorem spirat et ad redamandum provocat; caput inclinatum; manus expansae; pectus apertum*—His whole form breathes out love and provokes love in return; the head bowed down; the hands outstretched; the heart laid bare.

5. Charity is destroyed by mortal sin; it is *weakened* and its growth hindered by *venial sin*.

There is only one sin directly opposed to the love of God— *hatred of God*, the greatest of all sins, the sin of Satan and his followers.

B. The Virtue of Religion

1. The fruit of the three Theological Virtues is the moral virtue of Religion.

The word religion comes from the Latin verb *religare*, to bind. By religion, then, we are *bound to God*. Religion implies first a Supreme Being having sovereign sway over men and directing their destinies; it implies secondly that man, recognizing the existence of such a Being and feeling the need of His powerful help, freely subjects himself to Him and manifests that subjection by acts of homage and love, that is, by *worship*. When we do this habitually, we possess the *virtue of religion*.

Religion as a virtue is, therefore, a *quality of mind and heart which inclines us to pay to God the worship due to Him*.

Giotto

THE BETRAYAL

2. Three elements make up the complete notion of religion, the object, the motive, and the act of religion.— The *object* is God. The Blessed Virgin and the Saints are secondary objects because of their nearness to God and their intimate relations with Him.

The *motive* is our indebtedness to God and our complete dependence on Him.

The *act of religion* is worship, that is, the manner in which we acknowledge our indebtedness to God, our dependence on Him, and our love for Him.

3. The Worship of God a Strict Duty.— The following consideration will show that we have the *duty to worship God*:

God is our Creator, we are His creatures; He is our Lawgiver, we are His subjects; He is our Master, we are His servants. Therefore He has the right to demand from us honor, reverence, obedience, submission of mind and will, devotion and adoration; in a word, worship. But to rights correspond duties. Hence we have the duty to worship God.

4. We owe to God external as well as internal worship.— Not only in our hearts must we acknowledge and love the infinite majesty of God, but our internal homage must at times be manifested by external actions.

All worship of God must be "adoration in spirit and in truth," that is, it must correspond to the spiritual nature of God and proceed from our hearts. Purely external worship of God has no value whatever.

"The hour cometh and now is, when the true adorers shall adore the Father in spirit and in truth. For the Father also seeketh such to adore Him. God is a spirit, and they that adore Him, must adore Him in spirit and in truth" (John 4,23-24).

But *external worship* is neither superfluous nor worthless. Our Lord Himself took part in the public worship of the Jews in the Temple and in the synagogues. He only protested against abuses and disorders which disfigured the temple services (Matt. 5,23; 21,12).

It requires only a little reflection to make us see that external worship is necessary and obligatory:

a) We belong to God in body as well as in soul. Hence it is meet and just that we should pay homage to God with our outward as well as our inward faculties.

b) External worship is the natural complement of internal worship. We naturally and spontaneously give outward expression to our inward sentiments, and we often require outward means to arouse inward sentiments. Experience teaches us that the neglect of external acts of religion gradually leads to the extinction of the virtue of religion.

c) As members of society, especially as members of the great religious society, the Church, we are bound to practice our religion externally in order to give edification and good example.

d) By instituting the Holy Sacrifice of the Mass and the Sacraments Christ made it obligatory on all to worship God externally.

But doesn't Our Lord say: "When thou shalt pray, enter into thy chamber, and having shut the door, pray to thy Father in secret: and thy Father who seeth in secret will repay thee"? (Matt. 6,6.) Do not these words show that God does not want public worship?

We answer: The passage quoted does not treat of external worship at all. Our Lord's words are directed against the Pharisees who loved "to stand and pray in the synagogues and on the corners of the streets, *that they might be seen by men*," which was certainly conduct deserving reproof.

5. Acts of Religion.—When we honor God in Himself, our worship is *direct*; it is *indirect* when we honor Him in His Saints. Hence we distinguish direct and indirect acts of Religion. We shall treat of each separately.

1. Direct Acts of Religion

a) PRAYER

1. What is Prayer?—The simplest and most natural expression of worship is *prayer*. "Prayer is in Religion," says Novalis, "what thinking is in Philosophy." All intelligent creatures are bound to think about God and to hold converse with Him; in other words, to pray to Him. Prayer in this wider sense may be defined as a *raising of the heart and mind to God*; a conversation between the soul and God.

2. Kinds of Prayer.—Prayer may be purely *mental* or *vocal*, that is, expressed in language. Mental prayer or meditation is the application of the three powers of the soul to prayer. The *memory* proposes a religious or moral truth, the *understanding* considers this truth in its application to the person who meditates, and the *will* forms practical resolutions and desires grace to keep them. The practice of mental prayer is not necessary for salvation; it is.

however, a great and powerful help to self-improvement and advance in virtue.

3. The four great acts of prayer are *Adoration, Thanksgiving, Petition,* and, in the event of our having offended God, *Contrition.* The highest of these acts is adoration, by which we acknowledge God's supreme majesty and our entire dependence upon Him. The Book of Psalms furnishes the most sublime prayers of adoration and praise.

But as long as we are pilgrims here on earth, burdened with the cares and trials of life and uncertain of our eternal salvation, our prayers will be oftener prayers of petition, a calling to God from the depths. Even in those glorious hymns of adoration and praise and thanksgiving, the *Te Deum* and the *Gloria in Excelsis,* there are intermingled petitions for mercy and forgiveness. Our very word *prayer,* from the Latin *precari,* conveys the notion of petition. It is to the prayer of petition that the following remarks chiefly apply.

4. The objections so often made to prayer arise from two opposite errors—*chance* and *fate.* If all that happens takes place without any kind of power to regulate it (chance), or if everything is governed by rigid law which can not be controlled (fate), then of course it is useless to pray. But reason and revelation alike tell us that the world is ruled by the Providence of God. We firmly uphold the existence of law in the universe (the laws of nature), but at the same time we maintain that God, the author of this law, can counteract, suspend or change it at His pleasure. Thus we pray for rain, fine weather, or health because we believe that God is the Lord of heaven and earth, "who worketh all things according to the counsel of His will" (Eph. 1,11). *How* God brings about the answer to our prayers can not be exactly determined (*Catholic Dictionary,* Art. "Prayer").

"Prayers," says St. Thomas Aquinas, "may be efficacious with God without thereby infringing on the immutable order of Divine Providence, since, in the ordering of that Providence, the granting of this or that prayer offered by this or that individual has been taken account of from the beginning. We do not pray that the Divine dispositions in our regard may be changed, but that we may receive, in virtue of the Divine ordering, that which is the complement of our prayer."

ADORATION

"All the nations Thou hast made, shall come and adore before Thee, O Lord: and they shall glorify Thy name." (Ps. 85: 9.)

5. Why We Pray.—We pray to God, not because He does not know our needs, but because *it is His expressed wish that we should ourselves put them before Him.* Although Our Lord said: "Your Father knoweth that you have need of these things" (Matt. 6,32), yet He also told us "that we ought always to pray and not to faint" (Luke 18,1); and the great prayer which He Himself composed for us contains a number of specific petitions.

6. What may we ask for in prayer?—St. Augustine lays down the general rule that "we may pray for whatever we may lawfully desire." Hence we may ask for temporal as well as spiritual favors. According to St. Augustine we should pray for all men. We are bound to help our neighbor on the road to salvation, and prayer is one of the most powerful means of doing so. We are bound to pray for our *enemies* in general, that is, we are never allowed to exclude them from our prayers. Our Lord *counsels* us to pray for them specially: "Pray for them that persecute and calumniate you."

Bellini

ST. JEROME IN MEDITATION

Feuerstein

"Give us this day our daily bread."

7. How We Should Pray.—Since prayer is a speaking with God, it is evident that it should be performed with *attention and devotion.* Merely to pronounce a certain form of words is no prayer. "This people honoreth Me with their lips, but their heart is far from Me" (Matt. 15,7).

There are three kinds of attention: to the words, to the meaning of the words, and to the objects of the prayer, that is, to God and what we pray for. It is this last kind of attention that is required. Now it is by no means easy to keep our attention fixed on unseen objects. Hence the many *mind-wanderings, or distractions* to which we are liable during prayer. If these distractions are not willful— and they are not willful if we *try* to fix our attention on God— they are not sinful, and our prayer is not without fruit. If we wish to pray with attention we must prepare for prayer by collecting our thoughts. "Prepare thy soul for prayer, and be not as a man that tempteth God" (Ecclus. 18,23).

8. Successful Prayer.—Besides attention and devotion, the requisites of successful prayer are:

a) Fervor and perseverance. We must want intensely what we ask for. Such prayers were always heard and blessed by Our Lord here on earth. It was no listless, half-hearted cry that was uttered by the Syro-Phenician woman, or by the blind man at Jericho, or the Centurion, or the leper, or Martha and Mary.

b) Confidence. Never yet has a prayer fallen to the ground that went up from a trusting heart. The will to pray is always from God, and it is a pledge of His willingness to hear our prayer—

> Fervent love
> And lively hope with violence assail
> The kingdom of the heavens, and overcome
> The will of the Most High; not in such sort
> As man prevails o'er men, but conquers it
> Because 'tis willing to be conquered—still
> Though conquered, by its mercy conquering.
> —Dante, *Paradiso,* 20.

c) Gratitude. Gratitude is inseparable from confidence and humility. To acknowledge that all we have received in the past is from God, is to proclaim that we look to Him alone for the future. *"Be anxious for nothing, but in all prayer and entreaty, with thanksgiving, let your requests be made known to God"* (Phil. 4,6).

d) All our praying must be done *in the name of Jesus,* that is,

"In the name of Jesus, every knee shall bow."
(*Phil. 2: 10.*)

in living union with Him and in His spirit. Then our prayer is
infallible. But we cannot pray in the name of Jesus, unless we
are really united with Him by sanctifying grace, and filled with
His spirit: with humility and confidence and resignation to God's
will.

b) LITURGICAL PRAYER AND SACRIFICE; KEEPING HOLY THE LORD'S DAY

1. Origin of the Liturgy.—The consciousness that "many are
one body" (1 Cor. 10,17), that all Christians are members of the
mystical body of Christ, necessarily broadens out individual prayer
into *collective prayer*. From this consciousness, too, was born and
gradually developed that "year long dramatic action," the drama of
the Redemption—in other words, the *Liturgy*, or public worship
of the Church.

"Newman well said that, if Protestants but knew the Breviary, they could not think so ill of the Church that devised a prayer so beautiful. Non-Catholics have indeed often loved, often also imitated the rites and ceremonies of our Church. Every need of the human soul is there expressed and finds there besides expression, satisfaction. Every sort of worship ever devised by the human spirit has its purified analogue in our liturgy. Truth is expressed in beauty equivalent, inexhaustible depths of meaning are contained in the hallowed words and actions. In the liturgy, deep indeed calls to deep, the deep of the human heart to the deep of the Divine Being, revealed therein now in one, now in another of His attributes. The *lex credendi* is set forth in a *lex orandi* so persuasive that it must needs conciliate all who have eyes open to the beauty of holiness. Walter Pater speaks of it thus: 'All those various offices which in Pontifical, Missal, and Breviary, devout imagination had elaborated from age to age with such a depth of spiritual idea and light and shade, with so much poetic tact in quotation, such a depth of insight into the Christian soul, had joined themselves harmoniously together in this perpetual worship of the Mother of Churches'. But even these glowing words are cold to the reality. Indeed, I should almost dare to say, did the Church lack any other credentials whatever, her Divinity would be proved by her liturgy alone. Only the Holy Spirit could have accomplished a work so marvelous" (WATKINS, *Some Thoughts on Catholic Apologetics* [St. Louis: B. Herder Book Co.], p. 132).

2. The center and the soul of the public worship of the Church is the Holy Sacrifice of the Mass.—At this most sacred function the eternal High Priest Himself stands in the assembly of the faithful, in order to offer sacrifice for them and make intercession for them. At the altar all the barriers of time and space that separate the "three great provinces of the kingdom of God," the Church militant, suffering, and triumphant, are removed, each taking part, according to its needs and powers, in the blessings of the Eucharistic Sacrifice.

3. The Obligation of Hearing Mass.—Because the Mass is the sublimest of all forms of worship and for the individual soul the source of the richest blessings, the Church gathers the faithful around her altars on all Sundays and Holy-days for the celebration of the sacred mysteries, and *obliges them under pain of mortal sin to be present*, unless weighty reasons excuse them.

4. Sunday Rest.—In order to enable her children to take part in her liturgy on Sundays and Holy-days the Church, since the days of Constantine the Great, has forbidden all *servile work* on these days, that is, all bodily work which is commonly performed by servants, hired hands, day-laborers, and tradesmen.* The Day of

* The 1983 *Code of Canon Law* specifies that the types of work forbidden are those "which impede the worship to be rendered to God, the joy which is proper to the Lord's Day, or the proper relaxation of mind and body." (Can. 1247). —*Editor*, 1990.

THE MYSTERY OF FAITH

"For as often as you shall eat this bread and drink the chalice, you shall show the death of the Lord," (I Cor. 11: 26.)

the Lord should be a day of rest, sanctified by works of piety and charity. The Sunday rest, the Sunday dress, and the Sunday liturgy should remind us that we are children of God, called by Him to share one day in His own eternal Sabbath Rest (Heb. 4,10).

A Christian Sunday is a blessing; a Sunday passed in bad company in drunkenness, in impurity, in sinful amusements, is a curse to the individual and to society. What St. Augustine says of many Christians of his day, may well be applied to many more of our own day: "It would be better for them to dig all day on Sunday than to dance all day."

c) OATHS AND VOWS

1. Taking an Oath (swearing) means calling upon the all-knowing God to witness that we are speaking the truth or that we intend to keep our promise.

From this definition it is clear that an oath is an *act of Religion*, for by it we acknowledge God as the All-wise who knows our most hidden thoughts or intentions, as the All-truthful who can never sanction falsehood, as the All-just who will punish us if our words do not agree with our thoughts and intentions.

2. The lawfulness of taking an oath has been questioned not only by certain religious sects, such as the Quakers and Mennonites, but also by some Fathers of the Church. The opponents of the oath base their opposition on the words of Christ: "You have heard that it was said to them of old, Thou shalt not forswear thyself, but thou shalt perform thy oaths to the Lord. But I say unto you not to swear at all. . . . Let your speech be yea, yea: no, no, and that which is over and above these is of evil" (Matt. 5,33-37).

Our Lord's words are directed against the fraudulent oaths of the Pharisees (see Matt. 23,16-22). There is no question of oaths before a court of justice or a person in authority, but only of promissory oaths. Christ demands that in daily intercourse a Christian's character should make his word as good as his oath. "What is over and above this *is of evil*," since it is made necessary by the present evil condition of men, through which our trust in the truthfulness of our fellow-men is shaken. Christ did not mean to condemn the taking of an oath under all circumstances. He Himself answered without protest when Caiphas put Him under oath. St. Paul, far from contenting himself always with a simple yes or no, most distinctly calls God to witness the truth of his assertions (Rom. 1,9; Gal. 1,20; 2 Cor. 1,23).

3. The Church has always taught the lawfulness of oaths, provided that they are taken (*a*) with *judgment,* i.e., for a grave cause; (*b*) in *justice*, i.e., that the thing sworn be lawful, and (*c*) in *truth*, i.e., that the thing sworn be true. "Thou shalt swear in truth, and in judgment and in justice" (Jer. 4,2).

4. Since an oath is an act of Religion and of such great importance for human society, it should be taken only seldom and only when there is a real necessity.

It is a *sacred duty* to keep an oath, if we have sworn to do something that is lawful; but if we have sworn to do something that is sinful, we are not allowed to keep our oath.

5. A false oath or perjury is one of the greatest crimes, because it mocks the all-knowing God, destroys faith and confidence among men, and is often a cause of injury to others.

Persons who from religious scruples refuse to take an oath, should never be forced to do so: their word should be taken as their oath. In courts of justice it might be better never to put anyone under oath, but to punish a deliberately false statement just as severely as perjury is now punished.

6. A Vow is a free and deliberate promise made to God to do a good work and intended to be binding under pain of sin.

That such an act belongs to the virtue of Religion is clear from the fact that we thereby acknowledge the supreme dominion of God, and profess our submission to Him.

It is to God alone that a vow is made; to vow to a saint means to vow to God in honor of a saint.

From the earliest times vows have been taken. The Old Testament mentions them repeatedly. It is said of St. Paul in the Acts of the Apostles that he had a vow.

The *obligation* resulting from a vow is evident from its very nature. For if a man is bound to fulfill his promises to his fellowmen, how much more his vows to God.

7. The obligation of a vow ceases

a) When its fulfillment becomes impossible, useless or unlawful. A *real* vow, that is, one by which a *thing* is promised to God, is binding also upon the heirs of the person who has taken the vow.

b) By the intervention of one who commands the will of the person who has taken the vow. Hence the vows of children under age may be annulled by their parents.

c) By lawful dispensation for just causes.

The person who has taken the vow is always at liberty to change it into a more perfect one. The person who can dispense from a vow can also change it into a less perfect one.

A vow is such a serious and sacred thing that no one should bind himself by vow except after mature deliberation and, as a rule, only with the consent of the confessor.

d) SINS AGAINST THE VIRTUE OF RELIGION

The sins against the Virtue of Religion are of three kinds: (1) those that positively dishonor God; (2) those that transfer the honor due to God to other objects, and (3) those that pay honor to the true God but in an unbecoming way.

1. Acts by which God is positively dishonored are:

a) *Blasphemy*, or the employment of language (gestures or actions) dishonoring to God. It implies a *conscious and intentional* use of language which the speaker knows to be injurious to God. So called "profane swearing," culpable as it may be, is not blasphemy, because the intentional contempt of God is not there. In the Old Testament persons found guilty of blasphemy were stoned to death.

b) *Cursing*, or calling upon God to inflict some evil on ourselves, on our neighbor, or on any of God's creatures. Deliberate cursing is a grievous sin against the honor of God and the love which we owe to our neighbor and all the creatures of God. If a curse is but a thoughtless expression, and no irreverence whatever is meant, it would be only at the most a venial sin.

c) *Profanity*, or speaking of what is sacred without due reverence, is more or less serious according as the profane words are, or are not, spoken out of deliberate contempt of what is sacred. (Do you know an act of reparation for profane language?)

d) *Sacrilege*, or the profanation of what is holy. It may be *personal*, *local* or *real*, according as it is directed against a person, a place, or a thing consecrated to God. Maliciously to strike or abuse a person consecrated to God by Holy Orders or by vow, would be *personal sacrilege*; bloodshed, impurity, or theft committed in a church or a cemetery, *local sacrilege*; to steal a sacred vessel or to turn it to profane use, to exercise a holy office without ordination, or to administer or receive the Sacraments unworthily, *real sacrilege*.

e) Related to real Sacrilege is the sin of *Simony*, which is the

Schnorr

HELIODORUS IS PUNISHED FOR ROBBING THE TEMPLE

buying or selling of spiritual things, sacred offices, and the like, for money. It is so called from the sin of Simon Magus, who offered money to the Apostles to induce them to give him the sacred power which they possessed (Acts 8,20).

2. Acts by which the honor due to God is transferred to others are, besides Idolatry:

a) *Divination*, or the explicit or implicit invocation of the evil spirit to obtain the knowledge of hidden things. Under Divination may be classed *Astrology*, the pretended science of foretelling future events by the situation and different aspects of the heavenly bodies; *Necromancy*, which consists in holding pretended communication with the souls of the dead; *Palmistry*, foretelling the future by the lines of the hand; belief in *Dreams* as foreboding the future; and *fortune-telling* of every description, if seriously practiced.

b) *Magic*, a so-called art by which men profess to do things contrary to the laws of nature. It consists in having recourse to the devil with the object of working wonders by his assistance.

3. Acts by which God is honored in an unbecoming manner may be grouped under the heading *Superstition*.

Superstition (from the Latin *super* and *stare*) literally means standing still over or by a thing, hence in religious awe and fear. It is defined as a *manner of divine worship contrary to the teaching and practice of the Church*, or simply a wrongful worship of God due to the introduction of false or superfluous elements. Common examples of superstition are the prayers promising an infallible answer to various requests; indulgences which have never been granted; miracles, visions, and revelations which have never taken place. The propagators of such abuses are often guiltless of *formal sin* either because of their stupidity or their mistaken zeal. The Council of Trent issued a special decree against abuses in this matter (Sess. XXV).

e) CHRISTIAN SCIENCE AND SPIRITISM

1. Christian Science is a form of worship and a system of healing "discovered" by Mrs. Eddy, of New Hampshire, in 1866. She claimed that her new religion was directly revealed to her. In 1875 she wrote a book entitled *Science and Health, with a Key to the Scriptures,* which is read aloud at every Christian Science Sunday service with the same marks of honor as the Scriptures.

According to this new revelation there is no such thing as disease or sin. "Disease is but an error of the mind, of mortal mind as distinguished from the Divine Mind. Mind is the only reality; matter has no being; our bodies are only phantasms of the imagination. It is fear that produces disease, or seems to produce it, for it has no reality. It is fear that produces colics and fevers. It is belief in the possibility of broken bones that actually breaks them, or seems to break them, for in reality there are no bones to be broken. There is no such thing as sin, for we and God are one; or better, man is the thought of God" (Hill, *The Catholic's Ready Answer*).

It is evident that Christian Science is not Christian; but what about its science? What are we to think about the cures attributed to the healing method of the Christian Scientists?

Some of them are undoubtedly genuine. But that is nothing surprising. There are certain *functional* diseases which are most effectually cured by the methods of the Christian Scientists. These methods are, however, by no means new. They have long been known to specialists in all parts of the world. "There was no need of Mrs. Eddy's producing a travesty of Christianity to prove that there are diseases of the body that have their root in the mind, and that the best way of curing them is by influencing the thoughts and feelings of the sufferers." All attempts by the Christian Scientists to cure *organic diseases* have proved complete failures.

Christian Science is, therefore, neither Christian nor scientific. What is true in its teaching and methods is not new, and what is new is not true. It is one of the numberless forms of modern superstition. Man is a "religious animal"; take away the true God, and he will fall down and adore anything.

2. Spiritism (also called Spiritualism) is the term used for the last fifty years for a supposed communication with the dead, and for the doctrines connected with such communications.

Under the form of *Necromancy* Spiritism is as old as civilization. Spiritistic practices have been traced amongst the ancient Egyptians, the Greeks, the Jews, the Hindus, and even the North American Indians and the Esquimaux. It is mentioned with abhorrence and condemnation in the Old Testament (Lev. 20,6; 1 Kings 28,3). In its present form it first appeared in the United States in the year 1848, whence it spread quickly all over Europe.

Spiritism claims that the "other world" is directly accessible to our world, not merely by one revelation made once for all and preserved in its integrity, not merely by Sacraments or the reception of supernatural grace, not merely by exceptional and abnormal apparitions very occasionally granted by direct Divine permission; but by constant communications from the spirits of the departed (Rev. R. H. Benson, *Spiritualism*).

These communications are made in a variety of ways; but for all of them there is required what is known as the *mediumistic faculty* on the part of at least one of the inquirers. The *medium* is a person, usually a woman, living in this world who, through his or her peculiar constitution is enabled to act as a channel between the two worlds. It is usually necessary for the medium to pass into a state of trance before any communications from the other world take place.

There are several ways in which the disembodied spirits are said to communicate with this world:

a) The spirit delivers messages through the mouth of the medium.

b) The spirit delivers messages through inanimate objects, sometimes by means of a pencil placed on paper or within locked slates, sometimes by means of raps upon the table or the walls of a room, sometimes by the use of an instrument called the *planchette* or *ouija board*.

c) The spirit clothes itself with a body for the occasion. This is called materialization, and is acclaimed the greatest triumph of Spiritism.

It is claimed by the Spiritists that there is in the human body a certain force or matter called "astral"; and a medium is a person from whom this substance can be easily detached. This astral substance is situated on the border line between matter and spirit, and is the means by which disembodied spirits can communicate with those still in the flesh. A number of such mediums have been discovered in recent times. Several prominent scientists have made experiments with them, but without arriving at any definite results.

What are we to think of Spiritism? Why has the Church condemned it?

We must distinguish between Spiritism as a science and Spiritism as a creed or religion.

a) Although an enormous amount of fraud has always accompanied the practice of Spiritism, we cannot ascribe all the phenomena to fraud. There is a considerable residue of well-observed phenomena which until now have baffled all attempts to explain them by natural laws.

The alleged messages from the spirit world, whether they be by voice or the hand of the medium, may be nothing more than the result of thought transmission of *Telepathy*, which appears to be an established conclusion of science.

Many eminent scientists who examined the *physical* phenomena, such as sounds, lights, the movement of objects, and the various forms of materialization, are not satisfied with the evidence presented in their favor. Each case must rest on its own merits.

b) As a *creed or religious system*, Spiritism is directly opposed to the teachings of Christianity.

"It professes to have its own revelation derived from communication with spirits. It claims that all space is peopled by the spirits of persons who once inhabited this or other worlds. Even when separated from the body these spirits retain an ethereal human form; they are of every degree of excellence and happiness according to their life in the flesh, but all are subject to the law of progress and capable of arriving at perfection; all are able to communicate with mankind" (*Catholic Dictionary*, Art. "Spiritualism").

Hence the Church has more than once condemned the practices of Spiritism, and declared it grievously sinful to have any part or share in them, or even out of curiosity to be present at spiritistic gatherings. She condemns in the strongest terms any attempt to communicate in this manner with the spiritual world, as contrary to the Divine Will.

Some Catholic writers account for the spiritistic phenomena by the action of the wicked spirits, but they fail to bring any solid proofs for their view. The alleged manifestations from the other world are for the most part so childish and nonsensical that they do little honor to the intelligence even of a "fallen angel." It is true that many of the so-called revelations are opposed to Catholic teaching, especially in regard to the future state, to hell, heaven and purgatory, but in every case they have been found to correspond to the religious bias of the mediums or their inspirers. Even if we have not as yet found a natural explanation of certain spiritistic phenomena, that is no reason to suppose them to be of preternatural or diabolical origin.*

2. Indirect Acts of Religion, or the Veneration of the Saints

The Church teaches that it is right and useful to venerate and invoke the Saints, especially the Blessed Virgin Mary, and to venerate their images and relics.

a) VENERATION OF THE SAINTS

1. It is right to honor the Saints.—

a) We honor virtuous men on earth, why should we deny honor to the Saints in Heaven, who practiced virtue in such a sublime degree?

b) By honoring the Saints we honor God Himself; for what the Saints are and have they owe to God.

c) God Himself honors the Saints more than we can ever honor them. "Where I am," says Our Lord, "there also shall My servant be; if any man minister to Me, him will My Father honor" (John 12,26).

d) From the first centuries the Angels and Saints were honored by the Church.

In a letter on the martyrdom of St. Polycarp (A.D. 167) the Church of Smyrna declared: "We adore the Son of God, but we honor His martyrs

*Evidence of the last several decades, especially connected with cases of diabolical possession, would indicate that spiritism (including use of ouija boards, etc.) does in fact involve calling on the devils, whether intended by the practitioners or not. —*Editor*, 1990.

THE SAINTS IN HEAVEN

"After this I saw a great multitude . . . and they cried with a loud voice, saying 'Salvation to our God, who sitteth upon the throne and to the Lamb.'" (Apoc. 7: 9, 10.)

as the disciples and followers of Our Lord, for their exquisite love of their king and master."

In his *First Apology* St. Justin Martyr writes: "We honor God the Father and the Son and the host of blessed spirits."

From the most ancient times the Church has instituted festivals, and built churches and altars in commemoration of the Saints.

2. It is useful for salvation to honor the Saints because this practice incites us to imitate their example and to strive to become like them, that we may also one day share their eternal happiness.

3. We must never confuse the honor we pay to the Saints with the Divine honor we pay to God alone.—

a) We honor and adore God alone as our sovereign Lord and the Author of all good things; we honor the Saints only as His faithful servants and friends.

b) We kneel down, it is true, when we venerate the Saints; but we do not adore the Saints any more than a courtier adores his king when on his knees he asks a favor of him.

c) We consecrate churches and altars, and offer the Holy Sacrifice to God alone, although at the same time we honor the memory of the Saints and implore their intercession.

d) We honor God for His own sake, on account of the infinite perfection which He has of Himself; we honor the Saints on account of the gifts and advantages which they have received from Him.

b) INVOCATION OF THE SAINTS

The Invocation of the Saints is Useful and Salutary.—

a) We often ask our earthly friends to pray for us, and we have abundant warrant in the Scriptures for so doing. St. Paul writes: "I beseech you, brethren, for the Lord Jesus Christ's sake, that you strive together with me *in your prayers to God for me*" (Rom. 15,30). But if it is a Christian duty to ask a friend on earth to pray for us, why should we not request the same friend, when he has left the earth to pray for us in Heaven? Death does not dissolve the union between us.

b) Scripture teaches that the Angels and Saints in Heaven are aware of what happens to us here and pray for us. "There is joy in Heaven," says Our Lord, "in the presence of the Angels over one sinner that repenteth" (Luke 15,10). The Prophet

Jeremias, long after his death, "prayed much for the people, and for all the Holy City" (Mach. 15,14). "When thou didst pray with tears, I offered thy prayer to the Lord," said the Angel Raphael to Tobias (12,12).

c) God grants us graces and favors through the intercession of the Saints, because it is His Will that we should acknowledge our own unworthiness and the merits of His faithful servants. Therefore He Himself in former times commanded the friends of Job, saying: "Go to my servant Job, and my servant Job will pray for you" (Job 42,8).

d) From time immemorial it was customary in the Church to invoke the Saints. In the Roman Catacombs, particularly on the tombs of the martyrs, we find inscriptions appealing to the deceased to remember their friends on earth. One of them reads as follows: "Ask for us in thy prayers, for we know thou art with Christ."

St. Augustine says that, while in the Mass we commemorate other departed souls in order to *pray for them,* we invoke the martyrs that they may *pray for us.*

It is no mark of distrust in Jesus Christ when we address ourselves to the Saints, for we expect all grace and salvation from God alone through the merits of Jesus Christ. "There is one God, one mediator of God and man, the man Jesus Christ, who gave Himself a redemption for all" (1 Tim. 2,5). If the invocation of the Saints were a mark of distrust, St. Paul would not have asked the faithful to pray for him (Rom. 15,30); nor would St. James have written: "Pray for one another, that you may be saved; the continual prayer of a just man availeth much" (5,6).

AN INSCRIPTION ON A TOMB IN THE CATACOMBS

e) The difference between our praying to God and our praying to the Saints is clearly brought out in all the *Litanies*. We say: God the Father of Heaven, *have mercy on us;* but, Holy Mary, *pray for us.*

"Let us, then, learn," says Cardinal Manning, "that we can never be lonely or forsaken in this life. Shall they forget us because they are 'made perfect'? Shall they love us less because they now have power to love us more? If we forget them not, shall they not remember us with God? No trial, then, can isolate us, no sorrow can cut us off from the *Communion of Saints*. Kneel down, and you are with them; lift up your eyes, and the heavenly world, high above all perturbation, hangs serenely overhead; only a thin veil, it may be, floats between. All whom we loved and all who loved us are ever near, because ever in His presence, in whom we live and dwell."

c) SPECIAL VENERATION OF THE MOTHER OF GOD

A higher degree of veneration, above all the Angels and Saints, is due to the Mother of God.—

a) Christ Himself honored her in a special manner.

b) The Archangel Gabriel greeted her with the words: "Hail, full of grace. The Lord is with thee; blessed art thou amongst women."

c) St. Elizabeth cried out in awe and reverence: "Whence is this to me, that the Mother of my Lord should come to me?"

d) Mary's prophetic words: "From henceforth all generations shall call me blessed," have been unceasingly fulfilled throughout the history of the Church.

e) Mary alone, of all her race, was privileged to *co-operate* in the work of Redemption by her own free will and choice: "Behold the handmaid of the Lord; be it done to me according to thy word."

f) Christ was obedient to His Mother here on earth, and He surely will not refuse her anything now that she is with Him in Heaven.

The beneficial influence of the Blessed Virgin in the history of Christianity can hardly be exaggerated. "The world is governed by its ideals," writes the Rationalist William Lecky, "and seldom or never has there been one which has exercised a more salutary influence than the mediaeval conception of the Virgin. For the first time woman was elevated to her rightful position, and the sanctity of weakness was recognized, as well as the sanctity of sorrow. No longer the slave or toy of man, no longer associated only with ideas of degradation and of sensuality, women rose, in the person of the Virgin Mother, into a new sphere, and became the object of a reverential

THE MOTHER OF GOD

Botticelli

homage, of which antiquity had no conception. A new type of character was called into being; a new kind of admiration was fostered. Into a harsh and ignorant and benighted age this ideal type infused a conception of gentleness and purity, unknown to the proudest civilizations of the past. In the pages of living tenderness, which many a monkish writer has left in honor of his celestial patron; in the millions who, in many lands and in many ages, have sought to mould their characters into her image; in those holy maidens who, for the love of Mary, have separated themselves from all the glories and pleasures of the world, to seek in fastings and vigils and humble charity to render themselves worthy of her benediction; in the new sense of honor, in the chivalrous respect, in the softening of manners, in the refinement of tastes displayed in all the walks of society; in these and in many other ways we detect its influence. All that was best in Europe clustered around it, and it is the origin of many of the purest elements of our civilization."

d) THE VENERATION OF IMAGES

1. We Honor Images of Christ and the Saints:

a) because by honoring these we honor Christ Himself and His Saints;

b) because the contemplation of these images moves us to love and imitate Christ and the Saints.

2. The Council of Trent (session 25) gives clear and definite instruction on the question of the veneration of images:

"The images of Christ and of the Virgin Mother of God, and of the Saints are to be had and retained particularly in temples, and due honor and veneration are to be given them; *not that any divinity or virtue is believed to be in them on account of which they are to be worshipped, or that anything is to be asked of them, or that trust is to be reposed in images,* as was of old by the Gentiles, who placed their hope in idols; but because the honor which is shown them is referred to the prototypes which these images represent; so that we through the images which we kiss, before which we uncover the head or bend the knee, adore Christ and venerate the Saints, whom they represent. If any abuses have crept in among these holy and salutary observances, the Holy Synod ardently desires that they may be utterly abolished."

From this statement it follows that the Church gives to images an *inferior and relative honor,* so far as they relate to Christ and the Saints, and are memorials of them. We may not pray *to* images, for they can neither see, nor hear, nor help us. In other words, praying to a picture or image is categorically forbidden. It should also be borne in mind that the Church does not *compel* her children to kneel or pray before any image or statue.

3. But, it may be objected, isn't the veneration of images contrary to Scripture?—Do we not read in Exodus 20,4-5: "Thou shalt not make to thyself a graven thing, nor the likeness of anything. . . . Thou shalt not *adore* them nor *serve* them"?

The restriction added shows in what sense the making or possession of images was forbidden, viz., *to adore and serve them.* God Himself commanded Moses to "make two Cherubim of beaten gold on the two sides of the oracle" (Ex. 25,18), and also to make a brazen serpent, and set it up for a sign, which was a figure of our crucified Redeemer (John 3,14).

4. We speak of the adoration of the Cross; is that a proper expression?

When we speak of the adoration of the Cross, we understand, not *absolute* adoration, which is due to the Godhead, but only *relative* adoration, which is directed to Christ: we adore Christ Himself as represented in His image. When we make the Stations of the Cross, we genuflect before each of the fourteen crosses, saying: "We adore Thee, O Christ, and we bless Thee, because by Thy Holy Cross Thou hast redeemed the world."

5. God has been pleased occasionally, as Catholics believe on good grounds, to glorify images of Christ and the Saints, and to grant special graces to those who honor these images. Because we feel ourselves animated to pray before these images with greater fervor and confidence, we sometimes *go on pilgrimages to these so-called miraculous images.* No Catholic is *obliged* to do so, nor is he obliged to believe that these images are miraculous.

e) THE VENERATION OF RELICS

Relics include the bodies of departed saints, fragments of their bodies, articles or portions of articles which they used, such as clothes, vestments, rosaries, and the like. The most famous of all relics is the true Cross.

1. The Veneration of Relics was solemnly approved by the Council of Trent, and the reason for this approval given: "The holy bodies of the martyrs and of others now living with Christ,—which bodies were once living members of Christ, and temples of the Holy Ghost, and which by Him are to be raised to eternal life and to be glorified,—are to be venerated by the faithful" (Sess. 25).

2. Reverence for the Relics of Martyrs is as old as Christi-

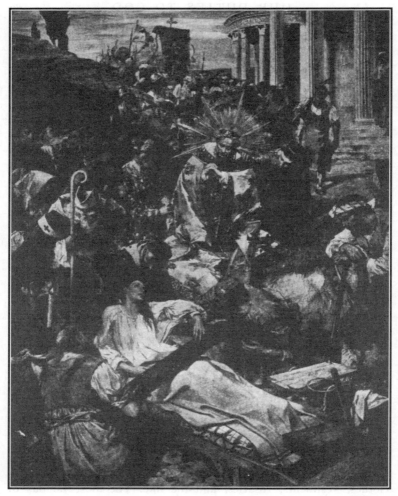

Feldmann

THE FINDING OF THE TRUE CROSS BY ST. HELENA

anity itself, and universal in the Eastern as well as the Western Church.

The Christians gathered the bones of St. Ignatius of Antioch (d. 107) and placed them in linen "as a priceless treasure, being left to the Holy Church by the grace which was in the martyr."

THE SANTA SCALA OR HOLY STAIRS

When St. Polycarp's body was burned in 167, the Christians gathered the bones they could find "as more precious than costly stones and more valuable than gold, and deposited them in a suitable place."

God is sometimes pleased to honor the relics of the Saints by making them instruments of healing and other miracles, and also by bestowing spiritual graces on those who with pure hearts, keep and honor them. In the Old Testament we read of the resurrection of a dead body which touched the bones of the prophet Eliseus (4 Kings 13,21), and we are told in the Acts of the Apostles that the sick were healed by towels which had touched the living body of St. Paul.

3. Abuses have occurred in all ages with regard to relics. The Fourth Council of the Lateran (1215) forbade relics to be sold or to be exposed outside of their cases or shrines, and prohibited the veneration of new relics till their authenticity had been approved by the Pope.

4. "He is not the God of the dead, but of the living; for all live unto Him."—These words of Christ to the Sadducees suggested to Cardinal Newman the following beautiful verses on the *Relics of Saints,* written in 1833 when he was still an Anglican:

> "The Fathers are in dust, yet live to God:"—
> So says the Truth; as if the motionless clay
> Still held the seeds of life beneath the sod,
> Smouldering and struggling till the judgment-day.
>
> And hence we learn with reverence to esteem
> Of these frail houses, though the grave confines;
> Sophist may urge his cunning test, and deem
> That they are earth;—but they are heavenly shrines.

SUGGESTIONS FOR STUDY AND REVIEW

A. The Three Theological Virtues

1. If we wish to attain our life's purpose, we must surrender ourselves completely to God, our First Cause and Last End. How is this surrender of ourselves accomplished? What is the fruit of this self-surrender?
2. Summarize the teaching of the Church on Faith:

   I. *Nature of Faith:* Make an *Act of Faith,* and you will see immediately in what Faith consists.

   II. *Qualities of Faith:* (a) Living; (b) Universal; (c) Conquering and Unconquerable. Give examples.

   III. *Cultivating Faith:* (a) Keep it alive; how? (b) profess it openly; when? (c) do not endanger it; (d) broaden and deepen it; how? (e) make Acts of Faith; why?

   IV. *Sins against Faith:* Explain each briefly in your own words. Illustrate your explanations with examples.

   V. *Dangers to the Faith and How the Church Tries to Safeguard Us against Them:* (a) Taking part in non-Catholic religious services; (b) Secret Societies; (c) Forbidden Books.

3. Make an *Act of Hope*. What threefold hope do we express in this prayer?
4. The virtue of Hope has been called the "homesickness of the soul after God." Comment on these words.
5. What qualities must our Hope have? Briefly explain each.
6. Why is *Despair* a most pernicious evil, and what are the surest remedies against it?
7. What do we understand by *Presumption*, and which are the best antidotes against it?
8. Often say the *Salve Regina*—Hail, Holy Queen; Mary is our Star of Hope in this valley of tears. Read the *Benedictus* (Luke 1,68-79). Why is it a "Canticle of Hope"?
9. Recall the story of Job. How did he console himself in his utter desolation? "I know that my Redeemer liveth. . . ." Hope in the resurrection.
10. Make an *Act of Charity*, or Love of God. What does it tell you about the *object* of Charity? the *motive* of Charity? Does it express perfect or imperfect love of God? An emotional love, or a love of preference?
11. Why is Charity called the Mother and Queen of virtues?
12. What qualities must our love of God possess?
13. How can we increase and perfect our love of God? How can the Crucifix aid us in perfecting our love of God?
14. Read St. Paul's "Canticle of Love," 1 Cor. 13 (Epistle for Quinquagesima Sunday).

B. The Virtue of Religion

Prepare a paper on "The Virtue of Religion," using the following outline:

I. Derivation of the word Religion. What two things Religion implies. What is Worship?
II. Definition of the virtue of Religion.
III. Three elements in the notion of Religion: *object, motive, act.*
IV. Worship of God a strict duty.
V. Why we owe *external* as well as *internal* worship to God.
VI. Acts of Religion: *Direct* and *Indirect.* Name the principal acts under each division.

1. *Direct Acts of Religion*

a) PRAYER

Prepare a paper on *Prayer*, using the following outline:

I. What is Prayer? Why is it the most natural expression of worship?
II. Distinguish between Mental and Vocal Prayer. Explain what Meditation is. Why is it so useful for spiritual advancement?
III. Which are the four great Acts of Prayer? Which is the highest, and why? Which is the most frequently used, and why?
IV. If God knows all things, why tell Him our needs?
V. What may we ask for in prayer?
VI. How should we pray? What about distractions?

VII. If we wish our prayers to be heard, what qualities should they have?

Prayer Without Words.—In the parish of Ars, in the time of its saintly parish priest, John Baptist Vianney, lived a simple peasant, poor and ignorant, but rich in piety and virtue. He was particularly remarkable for his devotion to Our Lord in the Blessed Sacrament. Whether going to work or returning from it, he never passed the door of the church without entering it to adore Our Lord. He would leave his tools on the steps, and remain for an hour or more sitting or kneeling before the tabernacle. The holy Curé, who watched him with delight, could never perceive the slightest movement of his lips. Being surprised at this circumstance, he said to him one day, "My good man, what do you say to Our Lord in those long visits you pay Him?"—"I say nothing to Him," was the reply; "I look at Him, and He looks at me" (*Life of St. John Baptist Vianney*).

Mule, Saddle, and Bridle.—St. Bernard was one day travelling with a simple countryman, who, noticing that the holy man kept his eyes modestly cast down during the journey, asked him why he did not look around at the beautiful scenery. The Saint answered that it was to avoid distractions in time of prayer. "Well," said the countryman, "when I pray, I pray; and when I travel, I look about." "Have you, then, no distractions at your prayers?" said St. Bernard. "None at all," answered his companion. "I do not believe it," the Saint replied. "Now let me make a bargain with you: If you can succeed in saying one *Our Father* without a distraction, I will give you this mule on which I am riding; if you do not succeed, you will come to Clairvaux and become a monk." The agreement was made, and the countryman began to recite the *Our Father*, but after a few words, he interrupted it and said: "Pray, Father, will you give me the saddle and the bridle too?" "Yes, I should have given you mule, saddle and bridle," said the Saint, "but because you have been distracted, you have lost all, and you must come with me to Clairvaux and become a monk."

b) LITURGICAL PRAYER AND SACRIFICE; KEEPING HOLY THE LORD'S DAY

1. What is meant by the *Liturgy*? Why is it called the "year long dramatic action"?
2. Why is the Holy Sacrifice of the Mass called the center and soul of the public worship of the Church?
3. Why does the Church oblige her children under pain of mortal sin to be present at Mass on certain days?
4. How should we spend our Sundays and Holy-Days? What is meant by *servile* work? Of what does the Sunday Rest remind us?
5. How is the Day of the Lord desecrated? What does St. Augustine say about dancing on Sundays?
6. Why do we keep holy the first day of the week and not the Sabbath, the seventh day, as God had commanded the Jews?

7. *Tom* makes his living by photography. He is poor, and in order to increase his meager income develops on Sundays the photographs taken during the week. Is he doing servile work and therefore transgressing the Third Commandment? Will necessity excuse him? Should he consult his pastor in this matter? (Before you decide this question, recall what is meant by servile work; namely, work that used to be done by slaves, and which is now done by servants and workmen, and which chiefly employs bodily strength. Common estimation and custom have much weight in deciding what is servile work. Mental or artistic work is not forbidden. Recall also who has dispensing power: the Pope for all the faithful; he can dispense any or all of the faithful from this law. Bishops can dispense their subjects in particular cases, as also can parish priests. Finally, remember that grave necessity excuses a person from the Sunday rest law without a dispensation.)

8. What are the conditions to be complied with in order to satisfy the precept of hearing Mass on days of obligation? List some valid excuses for remaining away from Mass on days of obligation. (Use your reason and common sense in deciding these matters, and in case of doubt consult your parish priest, your confessor, or any other priest.)

c) OATHS AND VOWS

1. What is an Oath? Show that it is an act of Religion.
2. Under what conditions does the Church permit the taking of an oath?
3. What kind of oaths did Our Lord oppose? Did He Himself take an oath?
4. Why is Perjury one of the greatest crimes?
5. *William*, a Quaker, is absolutely convinced that it is wrong to take an oath. Summoned as witness in a murder trial, he yields to pressure brought upon him by the judge and takes an oath. Does he commit a sin? Does the judge commit a sin by inducing him to take an oath?
6. What is a Vow? Show that it is an act of Religion.
7. To whom are vows made? *Clare,* a wealthy woman, makes a vow to St. Thérèse that she will build a shrine in her honor if her sick child recovers. Did Clare make a real vow?
8. What is the obligation imposed by a vow, and how does it cease?

d) SINS AGAINST THE VIRTUE OF RELIGION

1. Classify the sins against the virtue of Religion.
2. Explain briefly: *Blasphemy, Cursing, Profanity, Sacrilege and Simony.*
3. Give examples of *Personal, Local* and *Real Sacrilege.* When are they mortal sins?
4. Explain briefly: Divination, Astrology, Necromancy, Palmistry, Belief in Dreams, Fortune-telling, Magic. Show how by all these acts the honor due to God is transferred to creatures.
5. What is meant by Superstition. Give examples.
6. Distinguish between Superstition in the strict sense of the word and so-called "superstitious practices." Is fixing a horseshoe on the door to bring good luck superstition or a superstitious practice? (Superstitious

practices are practices which have no natural or supernatural connection with the end in view.)

7. Show the absurdity of all superstitious practices. (God provides for our wants in two ways: (*a*) by *natural* means, for example, food for supporting life, medicine for restoring health; (*b*) by *supernatural* means, e.g.: prayer, fasting, Sacraments, Indulgences, etc. Are these not sufficient for all our wants?)

e) CHRISTIAN SCIENCE AND SPIRITISM

1. If you care to acquaint yourself more thoroughly with Christian Science and Spiritism, consult the articles in the *Catholic Encyclopedia*, or the *Question Box*, pp. 23-26 and 402-404.

2. In what way does Christian Science conflict with the teachings of Christianity?

3. "What is true in Christian Science is not new, and what is new is not true." Comment on these words.

4. Of Mrs. Mary Baker Eddy's book, *Science and Health, with a Key to the Scriptures*, Mark Twain says: "Of all the strange and frantic and incomprehensible and uninterpretable books which the imagination of man has created, surely this one is the prize sample."

5. Why are Catholics not allowed to go to Christian Scientists for treatment even though they do not accept their religious teachings?

6. What is meant by *Spiritism*? Show that it is not an invention of the 19th century.

7. Why does the Catholic Church forbid Catholics to have anything to do with Spiritism?

8. How can we account for the spiritistic phenomena? Could they be produced by the wicked spirits? Are they the result of fraud and deception? *The Fools' Tax.*—The wealthy and populous city of Alexandria in Egypt at one time had a law which required all astrologers to pay a heavy tax. This tax was known as the "Fools' Tax" because it was raised on the folly and credulity of those who consulted the astrologers. If all the astrologers, fortune-tellers, and other frauds had to pay a special tax nowadays, the financial returns to the State would be very considerable. The number of fools seems to increase with the age of the world. Whoever consults a fortune-teller is a fool whether he believes in fortune-telling or not: he is a fool if he believes in such nonsense, and he is a still greater fool if he pays for a thing which he knows to be nonsense.

2. *Indirect Acts of Worship, or the Veneration of the Saints*

1. Summarize the teaching and practice of the Church in regard to Veneration and Invocation of the Saints, especially of the Blessed Virgin, and in regard to the veneration of their Images and Relics:

    I. It is right to honor the Saints.

    II. It is useful for salvation to honor the Saints.

    III. Difference between the honor paid to the Saints and the Divine honor paid to God alone.

    IV. It is useful and salutary to pray to the Saints. Show that it is not a mark of distrust in Christ when we address ourselves to the

Saints. The difference between praying to God and praying to the Saints brought out clearly in the public prayers of the Church.

V. Why the veneration and invocation of the Saints is so consoling.

VI. Why a higher degree of veneration, above all the Angels and Saints, is due to the Mother of God.

VII. Show the beneficial influence of devotion to the Blessed Virgin in the history of civilization.

VIII. Give two reasons why we honor the Images of Christ and the Saints. The Council of Trent on the Veneration of Images.

IX. The Veneration of Images not contrary to Scripture.

X. Explanation of the expression: "Adoration of the Cross."

XI. So-called "miraculous Images."

XII. Relics. The greatest Relic. Why the Church approves the veneration of Relics.

XIII. How the early Christians honored the Relics of the Martyrs.

XIV. What precautions does the Church take to prevent abuses in regard to Relics? Does it really matter much whether the particular Relic which we honor be authentic? Remember that the reverence we pay is to the Saint. Example of the monuments to the Unknown Soldier. The particular soldier thus honored may have been a coward or a rascal. The honors paid are given to the soldiers who died for their country.

Readings:

a) *Question Box,* pp. 562-576.

b) *Imitation of Christ,* Bk. I, ch. 18: "Of the Example of the Saints."

2. Write a short paper on the *Magnificat,* using the following hints:

1. The author of the Magnificat. The occasion of its composition. (Luke 1,46-55). Its use in the Liturgy of the Church.

2. The Magnificat contains a prophecy. Specify it. What impression would this prophecy have made at the time, say, on the Roman Empress. Show how this prophecy has been fulfilled and is being fulfilled every day.

3. How is the *humility* of the Blessed Virgin revealed in the Magnificat?

4. "He hath put down the mighty from their seat." Find examples in Scripture and profane history in proof of this. Also for the words: "He hath exalted the humble."

5. The Magnificat is a song of praise on certain attributes of God. Point out these attributes.

CHAPTER II

Duties Towards Ourselves

After our duties to God come our duties to ourselves. We are nowhere commanded to love ourselves, because this precept is clearly written in our nature. Love for self, so God tells us, is to be the rule and measure of our love towards our neighbor.

Christianity demands a *well-ordered self-love,* a self-love which is subordinated to the love of God, which tends to secure our true happiness by seeking eternal goods before all else and temporal goods only in so far as they promote our eternal interests. *False self-love* puts self in the place of God. It is the fundamental vice of human nature and the source of every sin.

Well-regulated self-love implies duties to the soul and to the body; and since man has a supernatural as well as a natural life, it also implies duties in regard to the preservation and development of our natural as well as our supernatural life. What we can and ought to do for the sanctification of our souls, formed the subject-matter of Grace and the Sacraments; here we shall confine ourselves to the consideration of our duties to ourselves in the natural order.

I. DUTIES IN REGARD TO THE INTELLECT AND THE WILL

Being intelligent and free beings, we can attain our last end only by intelligent and free acts; and since we are bound to strive for that end, we are also bound to perfect the means by which it is reached, i.e., to *perfect our intellect and our will.*

1. Our intellect is perfected by knowledge of truth.— Hence *we have a duty to acquire certain truths.* Some of these truths are so necessary that without a knowledge of them we could not attain our last end, God. As human beings, therefore, our first duties toward ourselves are to know God and the means that lead us to God.

As Christians and Catholics we must know the teachings of our holy religion, and know them as thoroughly as our talents and opportunities permit.

After this comes the duty to know those things without which we could not fulfill the duties of our *station or vocation in life*. The higher the vocation to which we are called, the greater is our responsibility, and the greater our obligation to acquire the knowledge and culture befitting that vocation.

2. The education of the heart and the will must keep step with the education of the intellect. Not the quantity of our knowledge, but the *quality of our conscience* determines the value of our personality and the value of our efforts for the common good.

"What will it avail thee to be engaged in profound discussions concerning the Trinity, if thou be void of humility and art thereby displeasing to the Trinity? Truly, sublime words do not make a man holy and just but a virtuous life maketh him dear to God. I had rather feel compunction than know how to define it. Yet learning is not to be blamed, nor the mere knowledge of anything whatsoever, for that is good in itself and ordained by God, but a good conscience and a virtuous life are always to be preferred" (*Imitation of Christ*).

3. Safeguarding Our Reputation.—A certain measure of consideration amongst our fellow-men is necessary if our life is to be in any sense fruitful, hence it is our duty to take pains to insure it. "A *good name* is better than great riches; and good favor is above silver and gold" (Prov. 22,1).

Although we may, as a rule, make light of what others say of us, still we must exercise reasonable care to safeguard our reputation. If the honor of our family or of our calling is at stake, we are even in conscience bound to defend ourselves when our character is aspersed. Our best defense in all circumstances is a life without reproach before God and men. That was St. Paul's defense: "Our glory is this, the testimony of our conscience" (2 Cor. 1,12).

2. The Dignity of the Human Body

1. The body is the abode and the instrument of the immortal soul.—Through the bodily senses the soul receives the knowledge of the world; the organs of the body give life and form to the creative thoughts of the soul; through the body the soul exercises its royal dominion over God's visible creation. In the supernatural order the body possesses a still higher worth and dignity. It is the "conductor of divine grace," the "mediator between God and the soul." In the mystery of the Incarnation the body attained its highest glory: "And the Word was made flesh, and dwelt amongst us." Through Baptism the body becomes a member of the glorified Christ and a temple of the Holy Ghost. Faithful companions through life, the soul and the body are not to be separated forever after death. "He that raised up Jesus Christ from the dead shall quicken also your mortal bodies, because of His Spirit that dwelleth in you" (Rom. 8,11).

2. The Body Not an Idol.—But the Christian conception of the body is far removed from *deification* of the body so prevalent in heathen times and amongst our own neo-pagans. Truth, which reveals to us the high dignity and destiny of the body, teaches us also the curse of original sin, and the tragic conflict which has resulted from the rebellion of the first man against his Creator.

3. With regard to our body we have **positive and negative duties.** By positive duties we mean all those acts which we are morally bound to perform in order to preserve and promote the health of the body; by negative duties we mean those acts which we must avoid as injurious to life and health.

A. Positive Duties Towards the Body

a) FOOD AND CLOTHING

1. The body requires nourishment for its preservation, for its development, and for the performance of the tasks demanded of it. For this purpose God has placed a great variety of food and drink from the storehouse of nature at man's disposal. No kind of food or drink as such is forbidden to man. The vegetarian and the total abstainer may forego the use of meat or alcoholic beverages, but they have no right to ban them for others as sinful. All that God requires of us is that our food and drink be placed under the control of reason. "I eat and drink to live," Socrates used to say; "there are some people who live to eat and drink."

2. Fasting and Abstinence.—"Control of the palate and the stomach," a well-known educator once remarked, "is the A-B-C of character formation." Hence the deep pedagogical wisdom that underlies the laws of the Church in regard to *Fasting and Abstinence.*

Fasting was practiced in the Old Testament, and Our Lord Himself fasted forty days in the desert. In the early Church the Christians fasted on Fridays. Later on the Lenten Fast was introduced in memory of Our Lord's fast. In the Preface of the Mass for the Lenten season the reasons why the Church recommends and commands fasting are clearly and succinctly set forth: *"Qui corporali jejunio vitia comprimis, mentem elevas, virtutem largiris et praemia*—On those who chastise their bodies by fasting Thou dost bestow the restraining of evil passions, uplifting of heart, and the enjoying of virtue with its reward."

Hendrich

CHRIST IN THE DESERT

3. Days of Fast and Abstinence.—But the Church does not recommend unlimited fasting, as many saints practiced it, for she knows that a healthy and strong body is a desirable foundation for a healthy soul. Hence she has appointed certain days on which her children must fast under pain of sin:*

a) The forty days of Lent, from Ash Wednesday to Easter, the Sundays excepted.

b) The Ember Days: Wednesday, Friday, and Saturday (1) after the third Sunday of Advent; (2) after the first Sunday of Lent; (3) after Pentecost; (4) after the Feast of the Exaltation of the Holy Cross, September 14.

* According to the current norms, established in 1966 by Pope Paul VI, one is *obliged* to fast only on Ash Wednesday and Good Friday, and to abstain only on Ash Wednesday and the Fridays of Lent, though on all other Fridays of the year one must still either abstain or perform some other commensurate penance. —*Editor*, 1990.

c) The *Vigils*, or eves of the Feasts of Pentecost, the Assumption, All Saints, and Christmas.

Two things are required for the observance of the law of fasting: one full meal, and that not taken before midday.*

The obligation of fasting begins at the completion of the twenty-first year and ceases with the beginning of the sixtieth year. Nowadays many are excused from fasting because the Church does not intend people to injure their health. The causes which excuse from fasting are: sickness or infirmity, poverty, hard labor, lawful dispensation. We should always consult our confessor in this matter and abide by his decision. If we are dispensed from fasting, we should perform other good works.

The Church has also appointed certain days of *Abstinence*;** that is, days on which we must not eat flesh-meat or the juice of flesh-meat (soup, broth, etc.). These days of abstinence are: all the Fridays throughout the year, Ash Wednesday and all the other Wednesdays of Lent, the Ember Days, and the Vigils of the great feasts. On Holy Saturday abstinence ceases at noon. When a holy day of obligation outside of Lent falls on a Friday, or when a vigil occurs on a Sunday, there is no abstinence.

The law of abstinence is binding on all who are seven years*** old and over, unless they are lawfully excused by sickness, necessity, or dispensation. The violating of the law of fasting and abstinence is always of itself a grievous sin, though in a slight matter it may be only a venial sin.

4. More important still than temperance in eating is **temperance in the use of alcoholic beverages.** The abuse of alcohol is the cause of untold misery to the individual, the family, and the whole human society. So great indeed have the evil effects of excessive drinking become in our day that in several countries legal prohibition, in others state control of intoxicating beverages, has been established. But no amount of legislation can effect a reform. The virtue to be cultivated in drinking as well as in eating is temperance, that is, "the habitual use of the necessaries and the legitimate luxuries of life with that moderation and order which the law of God speaking through right reason dictates." "For the kingdom of God is not meat and drink; but justice. and peace, and joy in the Holy Ghost" (Rom. 14,17).

*Before "midday" no longer applies. —*Editor*, 1990.

**See footnote on page 101. —*Editor*, 1990.

***The law of abstinence now obliges those 14 and over. —*Editor*, 1990.

5. Clothing.—Just as neither food nor drink is primarily intended to be an instrument of pleasure, so neither is *clothing* intended to be an instrument of vanity and an incitement to sin. "The purpose of dress is twofold, to *protect* the body and to *ornament* it. Some women nowadays pervert the use of dress. It is the nature of woman to be attractive, but her greatest attraction should be her modesty. Any woman can attract by a certain style of dress or lack of dress, but it is not the attraction that a Christian woman cares for.

"It is not only religious people who lament the indecency of modern dress. Physicians, statesmen, and moralists join in the condemnation of the present immodest fashions. They condemn them because of their positive harm. Dr. Foveau de Courmelles, one of the best-known physicians in Europe, declares that some of the worst evils confronting civilized nations may be laid at the door of the feminine craze for indecent dress.

"Man has a twofold nature, animal and spiritual. An immodestly dressed woman may win the admiration of man's animal nature; but it is a brutal admiration, not only not worth having, but positively dangerous to both man and woman.

"It is because the Catholic Church seeks the true welfare of women that it insists so much on modesty of dress. The womanly qualities that attract the *true love* of a man are those not dependent on an unseemly display of the person. And if a woman does not win the true love of a man she had better a thousand times remain single."—MARTIN SCOTT, S. J., *You and Yours* (New York: P. J. Kenedy & Sons), pp. 112-114.

b) RECREATION AND AMUSEMENT

1. For the preservation of bodily health and vigor we need more than food and clothing; we also need **periods of rest and recreation.** Pleasures and enjoyments are in some degree as needful for us as the air we breathe or the food we eat. Some people think that piety must be gloomy and religion stiff and repelling. Christ did not think so. At the very opening of His ministry to man we find Him with His Blessed Mother and His disciples sanctifying by His presence the marriage feast of Cana—not merely tolerating, but by a miracle promoting and approving harmless mirth and conviviality.

2. Morality of Amusements.—It is hard to lay down specific rules in regard to the various forms of recreation and amusement, such as theaters, movies, dances, socials, games, sports. "But on one thing we can be specific. If we find that any game or diversion is the *cause or occasion of sin* for us, we should drop it. If, after any amusement, we feel less like looking into the face of God, or our own mother, we should keep away from it thereafter. The principal purpose of amusement is to give rest and recreation to fit us for the burdens of life. If we find that a certain recreation interferes with our duties, our responsibilities, our self-respect, we should let it alone" (*You and Yours,* p. 172).

B. Negative Duties Towards the Body

If we have the positive duty to use our body according to the intentions of our Creator, it follows that all actions which are injurious to health, or which involve abuse or mutilation of the members of the body or the destruction of life itself by suicide are morally forbidden. We shall consider the gravest of these sins first.

a) SUICIDE

1. He commits suicide who freely and deliberately brings about the destruction of his own life.

Suicide was almost unknown during the ages of Faith. Since the fifteenth century it has become more and more frequent, until in our own day the yearly number of suicides in the chief countries of the world amounts to many thousands.

The *motives* of suicide are manifold. Despondency, business loss, insanity, ill health, disappointment in love, domestic troubles, fear of disgrace, grief, alcoholism, are amongst the motives which recur most frequently. Irreligion and moral depravity are commonly at the root of the evil. When a person loses the strong support of the Christian faith, he is helpless in the struggle with the ills and misfortunes of life.

2. Direct and deliberate suicide is always a mortal sin.—
a) Suicide is a *crime against God,* who alone gives life and determines its duration, and who has solemnly declared: "Thou shalt not kill."

b) Suicide is a *crime against one's own soul,* which is violently thrust out of that position which has been assigned to it by the Creator. Christianity gives the Christian the means to bear the hardest blows of fortune and to expiate the gravest crimes.

c) Suicide is a *crime against human society,* which it unjustly deprives of one of its members.

Hence we may easily understand why the Church denies

Christian burial to those who voluntarily and while in full possession of their faculties put an end to themselves. Still in such cases the law of the Church inclines to lenient judgment. Thus if a person be found drowned or poisoned, and if it be not proved that he had expressed the deliberate intention of committing suicide, some other cause of death, such as murder, accident, or temporary insanity, is presumed, and Christian burial is not refused.

b) INDIRECT SUICIDE AND RISKING ONE'S LIFE

1. Direct suicide must not be confounded with *indirect suicide*. An example of indirect suicide would be the action of a soldier in battle who charges a strongly fortified position of the enemy, or of a person who jumps from a boat in mid-ocean to save the life of another person. If death follows in these and similar cases, it is in no wise criminal. Such a death may constitute an heroic act of virtue; it may even be a duty.

2. It is unlawful without sufficient cause to expose one's life to danger.—Serious risks of life that are taken in a spirit of bravado or merely to win fame or money, are unlawful. On the other hand, it is lawful to risk one's life

a) if the action is good or at least indifferent and at least as liable to be safe as to be injurious; and

b) if one has an honest intention in undertaking the action and a good reason for assuming the risk of death or injury.

Hence miners, or steel workers, or employees in munitions factories, or aviators, may legitimately engage in these occupations under the above conditions.

3. Since parts exist for the whole, God's law demands that we preserve our limbs as well as the body itself. Hence it is lawful to submit to the amputation of a hand or a foot, or to any other mutilation *only when the well-being of the whole body demands it;* otherwise it is criminal. One is never obliged in conscience to undergo a surgical operation involving danger of death.

4. Dueling, which may be defined as a premeditated combat between two persons for the purpose of deciding with *deadly weapons* some private difference or quarrel, is *strictly forbidden by the Church*. The Council of Trent excommunicated all who engaged in duels, and those who counseled or promoted them, besides depriving persons who died in a duel of Christian burial (Session xxv,19).

5. **If we desire death** in order to be at rest with God, we desire a good thing, and such a desire is meritorious. "I desire to be dissolved and to be with Christ," says St. Paul. If we desire death with the sole view of escaping the ills and troubles of life, our desire is also good, but less meritorious. But if we desire death in opposition to God's Providence and in rebellion against His will, our desire is a *grievous sin.*

c) CREMATION

1. Christian Burial.—Not only during life, but also after death the Christian treats the human body with respect and reverence. Faith in the resurrection tells him that the separation between the soul and the body will be only temporary. Mindful of the words spoken by God to the first man: "Dust thou art and unto dust thou shalt return"; mindful also of the Savior's own burial and resurrection, the Church has always, with solemn rites, consigned the mortal remains of her children to the earth in consecrated ground.

2. Cremation a Pagan Practice.—The custom of burning the bodies of the deceased is also very ancient; but wherever Christianity took root, *cremation* was abolished. In modern times efforts have been made to force this pagan practice on the world once more.

On December 8, 1869, the International Congress of Freemasons imposed it as a duty on all its members to do all in their power to wipe out Catholicity from the face of the earth. Cremation was proposed as a suitable means to this end, since it was calculated to gradually undermine the faith of the people in "the resurrection of the body and life everlasting." In the same year societies were founded in various countries to spread the practice of cremation.

3. On May 19, 1886, the Holy See declared it **unlawful to become a member of any cremation society,** or to leave orders for the burning of one's body or that of another. Ignorance of the law of the Church or inability to reverse orders given for cremation, may be a just plea for indulgence at the hands of the Church.

There is nothing intrinsically wrong in burning the bodies of the dead. The practice might become necessary after a battle or during a plague. But in ordinary times, as the decree above quoted declares, "cremation disturbs the pious sentiments of the faithful; it is not in keeping with the beautiful rites of Christian burial; and it has been introduced by the deadly enemies of the Church." These reasons certainly justify its condemnation.

3. Chastity and Its Violation

1. Purpose of the Sexual Powers.—The social unit of mankind is the family; in other words, the human race is built up of families as a house is built of bricks, or living tissue of cells; and the family rests on the institution of *marriage*—a divine institution from the beginning and raised to the dignity of a Sacrament by Christ.

God has put into man's nature certain powers, passions, instincts, meant to be used in the holy state of Matrimony. If the sexes were without these instincts, if man and woman were not strongly and agreeably drawn to each other, there would be no marriage, and the human race would perish. Since these powers and instincts were given by God for the purpose of establishing the family and continuing the human race, they must be kept for that purpose only; to use them in any other way, merely for our own pleasure and satisfaction, would be a grave sin against nature and the will of God expressed in the *Sixth and Ninth Commandments.*

A reasonable curiosity about these powers implanted in our nature by God is quite right and natural, and if young people feel themselves unduly ignorant they should seek information from their parents or some older person whom they trust (Drinkwater, *Twelve and After,* p. 96).

2. Marriage and Celibacy.—Although God Himself instituted marriage for the conservation of the human race, still not all are obliged to marry. Many are debarred from marrying, others remain single of their own free will. Whoever chooses the state of *celibacy or virginity* for some higher end, that is in order to devote all his time and energy to the service of God and his fellowmen, does something more pleasing to God than if he followed the natural impulse to marry (1 Cor. 7,25-36).

But the high value put upon celibacy by Christianity implies no disparagement of the marriage state. Christ, who was born of a Virgin Mother and whose intimate friend was a virgin disciple, worked His first miracle for the benefit of the bride and bridegroom at a marriage feast.

3. The virtue which regulates the sexual life of man is called Chastity.—
Chastity is derived from the Latin word *castigare*, to chastise. "By the virtue of chastity reason chastises the lust of the flesh which we should correct as we would a rebellious servant."

Chastity demands not only control of external acts, but also *purity of heart*; in other words, purity of thought and desire. "You have heard that it was said to them of old: Thou shalt not commit adultery. But I say to you, that whosoever shall look on a woman to lust after her, hath already committed adultery with her in his heart" (Matt. 5,27-28).

Chastity is a most beautiful virtue.—God Himself tells us that. "Oh, how beautiful is the chaste generation with glory: for the memory thereof is immortal, because it is known both with God and with men" (Wis. 4,1). It makes man even here on earth like the Angels of Heaven: "Blessed are the clean of heart," says Our Savior, "for they shall see God" (Matt. 5,8). It brings a delightful peace into the soul and infuses courage to do and to dare great things for God and our fellow-men:

> "My strength is as the strength of ten
> Because my heart is pure."

4. The sins opposed to the virtue of chastity are called sins of impurity—the sins forbidden by the Sixth and Ninth Commandments. The Sixth Commandment forbids all sins of impurity with another's wife or husband (adultery), and all other external acts of impurity with ourselves or others. The Ninth Commandment forbids all interior sins—of thought and desire contrary to chastity. We sin against this commandment whenever we consent to impure thoughts and desire their accomplishment; whenever we take pleasure in them without desiring their accomplishment; and whenever we are conscious of such thoughts or desires and willfully neglect to put them away.

5. Every sin against the virtue of chastity is a mortal sin when committed with full advertence and full consent of the will.—However, the guilt arising from adultery is far greater than an act of impurity between two unmarried persons, for in the former case there is added a grave breach of justice. Some sins, then, of impurity are more grievous than others, and may vary according to the persons with whom they are committed, and

St. John and Jesus

according as the sin is more unnatural, odious, and abominable.

6. Impurity desecrates our human dignity.—A man who does not ennoble the sexual appetite by the spiritual power of the will, sinks down to the level of the brute; and if he is given to unnatural impure practices, he sinks lower still. Impure lust, when once it is pandered to, grows ever more imperious and makes the vilest slaves of its victims. The resistance of the will grows weaker with every defeat, and complete loss of will-power often results. Nature, which is God's servant, takes an awful toll for the transgression of its laws. "The wages of sin is death."

The unchaste lose little by little all taste for religion and piety. The Apostle sees in the sin of impurity a violent rupture between Christ and the soul, a squandering of the price of our redemption, a desecration of the temple of the Holy Ghost, and a forfeiting of the eternal inheritance (1 Cor. 6,15-17; 6,19; 3,16-17; Gal. 5,19).

7. Impurity is a sin against human society.—It poisons the wellspring of life and undermines the foundations of society, which rest on the propagation of the human race in moral purity and strength, on marriage and the family. When it becomes a national vice, impurity spells ruin to whole states and peoples.

8. Like all things really worth possessing, the virtue of holy purity must be fought for.—We are never secure against the recurrence of temptations to impurity. We shall have to fight against evil thoughts and desires all the days of our life. There may be an occasional truce, but there is no lasting peace.

The fight against temptation and sin will be crowned with success only if we conscientiously make use of the means, natural and supernatural, placed at our disposal.

Schnorr

THE PROPHET DANIEL SAVES THE VIRTUOUS SUSANNA

Dürer

St. George

a) We must be temperate in eating and drinking; avoid idleness; shun bad company, indecent plays and dances and filthy literature; carefully guard our senses, especially our eyes—through one unguarded glance David became an adulterer and a murderer.

b) One of the most effective means of avoiding sin is a lively consciousness of *God's presence*. The soul hallowed by the consciousness of God's presence as naturally repels the assaults of the tempter as the eyelid closes when a speck of dust seeks entrance into the eye.

It was the consciousness of God's holy presence that gave the chaste Susanna the courage to risk her life rather than to lose her honor: "It is far better for me to fall into your hands without doing it, than to *sin in the sight of the Lord*" (Dan. 13,23). From the same source Joseph drew strength to resist the seduction of a depraved woman: "How can I do this wicked thing, and sin against my God?" (Gen. 39,9).

c) The special means of keeping the pearl among the virtues or of recovering it when lost is the *reception of the Sacraments*. The humble confession of sin takes away the burden of past guilt and fills the soul with fresh confidence and courage; Holy Communion, often and worthily received, gives the soul a taste of that heavenly peace which the slave of passion misses so sorely.

Young men are sometimes told by unscrupulous physicians and ignorant quacks that they must gratify their sexual appetites to keep themselves in health. This assertion has been refuted a thousand times. The Medical Faculty of the University of Christiania, Norway, categorically declares: "We know of no sickness or any infirmity whatever, of which it can be said that it resulted from a perfectly pure and chaste life." At the beginning of the World War Dr. McLaughlin, of the United States Health Service, declared publicly that "continence is compatible with health." Whoever maintains the contrary sins against health as well as against morals.

"And a path and a way shall be there, and it shall be called the holy way. The unclean shall not pass over it. The redeemed of the Lord shall walk there, and everlasting joy shall be upon their heads" (Is. 35,8).

4. DUTIES CONCERNING MATERIAL GOODS

a) The Right of Private Property

1. Ownership Defined.—Not only spiritual goods, but material goods also have been placed at the disposal of man by God. But whilst the goods of the soul and the mind are accessible to all and do not diminish, no matter how many partake of them, a material good can, of its very nature, belong undivided only to one person, and the oftener it is divided, the smaller becomes the portion of those who use it. The right to possess, enjoy, and dispose of any material good for ourselves, to the exclusion of all others, is called the *right of private property* or individual ownership.

2. Private ownership rests on the divine law and, taking men as they are, is necessary for the individual and for society.—

a) The Seventh Commandment forbids theft as a violation of the rights of others. If private property were theft, as the French Communist Proudhon calls it, theft would not be a violation of the right of our *neighbor,* but of the right of the *State.* But God does not forbid theft as a violation of the right of the State, but of the right of our neighbor individually; as He forbids adultery, not as a violation of the right of the State, but of the right of the individual: "Thou shalt not covet thy *neighbor's house*; neither shalt thou desire *his wife,* nor *his* ox, nor anything that is *his"* (Ex. 20,17).

In the New Testament parables such as those of the sower, the vineyard, and the fig-tree presuppose the right of private property. To the rich young man Christ says: "Go, sell what thou hast, and give to the poor." The young man could not lawfully sell his possessions, if they were not really his. And how could Christ have praised the publican Zacheus, when he declared himself ready to give one-half of his possessions to the poor, if they were not really his. Our Lord also incidentally mentions a number of *titles* to private ownership; He speaks of buying and selling, of wages and ownership.

b) Private ownership is founded on the nature and condition of man; it is a *natural right.* Nature imposes upon man the duty of preserving his life, and hence it also gives him the *right* to exclusive ownership in those things necessary for the preservation of his life.

c) The individual has natural duties to provide for the material needs of his family and the education of his children. But he cannot fulfill these duties without the right of accumulating and retaining a variety of these goods. If all men were perfect Christians, then the difficulty would be minimized. But we must take men as they are.

d) Without the right to private ownership there would be no incentive to work, and consequently no progress in the arts and sciences.

e) God is the true Lord and Master of all things by the right of creation. But man also, the image of God, can mould and modify things at his pleasure. The fruits of his labor bear the stamp of his personality; and thus he becomes their true lord in a limited sense, as God is their absolute lord in an unlimited sense.

f) Under a system of common ownership (Communism) the distribution of labor and of the rewards of labor would destroy individual liberty and make all citizens slaves of the State. Under such circumstances peace and order are inconceivable.

The Church has always defended the right of private property.—In the early ages the followers of a certain commu-

Doré

THE RICH MAN AND LAZARUS

nistic doctrine, who called themselves *Apostolics*, were numbered among the heretics. In the Middle Ages the Church condemned the doctrine of Wickliffe, who maintained that it was contrary to Scripture for the clergy to possess property. When, in 1926, the German Socialists wished to confiscate the private property of the dethroned German rulers without compensation, the German bishops branded this proceeding as "contrary to the natural and Christian moral law."

But it may be objected: Did not God grant the earth to mankind in general, as we read in Gen. 1,28-29, and not to individuals?

We answer with Pope Leo XIII: "To affirm that God has given the earth for the use and enjoyment of the whole human race is not to deny that private property is lawful. For God granted the earth to mankind in general, not in the sense that all without distinction can deal with it as they like, but rather that no part of it has been assigned to any one in particular, and that the limits of private property have been left to be fixed by *man's own industry and by the laws of individual races*."

3. Christ does not forbid us to seek material goods: "Your Heavenly Father knoweth that you have need of these things." But He wants us to seek them in due turn and measure, *after*, not *before*, the Kingdom of God. "Seek ye first the Kingdom of God."

Even the accumulation of riches is not in itself against the moral law. But there are so many dangers connected with the pursuit of wealth that Our Savior warns His followers often and earnestly against the desire of worldly wealth and inordinate attachment to it. Some Fathers of the Church, in holy anger against the hard-heartedness and injustice of the rich, made use of expressions, which, torn from their context, read like sweeping condemnations of all private property.

4. Whether we possess much or little, we must always remember that **we are only the stewards of what we possess, not the absolute masters,** and that we must one day give an account of our stewardship. For as God never gives up His dominion over the gifts of life, so He never relinquishes His right over the gift of material goods.

b) Capitalism and Socialism

1. Communism, Socialism, Capitalism.—*Communism* defends the *community of all material goods* under all circumstances. It would have the State own everything. *Socialism* would have the State own all the *instruments of production,* as lands, mines, machinery; and all the *instruments of distribution*, as railroads, steamships, factories, banks; in other words, Socialism is the foe of *Capitalism*, which is the system of privately owned means of production and distribution. We have already refuted communism by proving the right of private property. Here we are concerned with the two mortal enemies, who have been struggling for supremacy for nearly fifty years in most of the countries of the world.

2. Socialism Wrong.—Socialist leaders claim that it is their mission to improve the condition of the working classes. To attain this end, they say, public ownership must be substituted for the present system of private ownership of the means of production; this once accomplished, the laborer's lot would be vastly improved. In the Socialist commonwealth all men would be really equal and enjoy temporal felicity and independence.

That our present social conditions stand in need of improvement, no one will deny; but it is equally true that the means of improvement proposed by the Socialists are both unjust and practically impossible.

a) "Under Socialism the worker would be directly and constantly dependent upon the State, from the cradle to the grave.

BISHOP VON KETTELER
A Pioneer of Christian Social Reform

All his life he would be merely a hired man. He could become contented with this degenerate state only after he had lost all of that initiative, that self-respect and that ambition which are essential to our efficient and worthy human existence. Under Socialism he must work for the State or starve. Likewise he must buy the necessaries and comforts of life from the State, and be content with what the State sees fit to produce. The point is that in these vital matters the workers would be denied all *liberty* of *choice"* Rev. John A. Ryan, *The Church and Socialism* (New York: The Macmillan Company), p. 5.

b) Socialism is *unjust*, because it deprives both the individual and the family, which existed prior to the State, of the natural right to property.

c) Socialism is a *practical impossibility*. In the Socialist State the State would possess all land and all capital and distribute to each individual his portion of land and his occupation. But how could the State portion out work and profit according to the abilities and merits of each one without thoroughly knowing the strength, talents, abilities, aptitudes of each one, which is a thing impossible? "Would not the most serious complaints of unjust distribution be raised if one received fertile, another barren, land; if one received an honorable, another a lowly, occupation? The consequence would be that whenever one would achieve greater results than another, for the maintenance of equality a new distribution would have to be made yearly, or even daily, and thus grounds for fresh complaints would be given."

3. Menace of Capitalism.—It would be contrary to the Christian conception of private ownership to condemn *Capitalism* outright. It would be unjust to close our eyes to the advantages which have resulted from the present capitalistic or industrial system—from the use of machinery in production, the uniting of many hands under one general direction, the utilization of the physical sciences; from the thought, genius, enterprise and superior power of management and administration of the captains of industry.

But from the point of view of Christian morality we must condemn most emphatically the capitalism which subordinates the common welfare to its own insatiable hunger for gold, which knows no higher aim in life than the heaping up of wealth and the squandering of it in luxury. Such heartless Capitalism is the deadly enemy of humanity and of all the higher values of life; it is as materialistic in its principles as Socialism and, if unchecked, as great a menace to society as Bolshevism.

4. The State can do much, and in some cases has done much, to check the abuses of Capitalism; but **the key to the solution of the social question lies in the Gospel of Christ.** It is true, we shall look in vain in the teaching of Christ for explicit pronouncements on all the complicated questions indicated by the words Capitalism and Socialism. Christ was no social reformer, in our sense of the word. But wherever the Gospel of Christ—the Gospel of peace and good will to all men, the Gospel of justice and charity and mercy, the Gospel of the Beatitudes and the Our Father, the Gospel of the Blessed Eucharist, which draws all men together in "one Bread and one Body"—wherever this Gospel becomes a *fact,* the social question is automatically solved.

SUGGESTIONS FOR STUDY AND REVIEW

1. DUTIES IN REGARD TO THE INTELLECT AND THE WILL

2. THE DIGNITY OF THE HUMAN BODY

1. Why must we strive to perfect our intellect and our will?
2. How is our intellect perfected? What truths are we bound to acquire?
3. Why doesn't the quantity of our knowledge determine the value of our personality? What does the *Imitation of Christ* say on this matter?
4. Why is it our duty to safeguard our good name? Which is the surest means of doing so?
5. Why should we at all times have great reverence and respect for our bodies? Why should we not idolize our bodies, but keep them in subjection to our reason?
6. "A healthy soul in a healthy body." Comment on these words of an ancient sage.
7. Write a short paper, to be delivered before the class, on *Fasting and Abstinence,* using the following outline:
   1) Importance of Fasting and Abstinence for character formation.
   2) Fasting in the Old and New Testaments and in the early Church.
   3) The *Preface for the Masses of Lent* on the value of Fasting.
   4) Why the Church has appointed certain days on which her children must fast or abstain, or both, under pain of sin.
   5) When does the obligation of abstinence begin? when that of fasting? In what does each consist?
   6) Which days are days of fasting alone? which of abstinence alone? which of both fasting and abstinence?
   7) What is meant by "the Workingmen's Indult?"
   8) Who are excused from fasting? Who can dispense? (Bishops and pastors.)

9) What is meant by the "Eucharistic Fast"?

I. *No one may eat meat on*
   a) All Fridays;
   b) Ash Wednesday;
   c) Wednesday of Holy Week;
   d) Christmas Eve.

II. *Workingmen and members of their household* may eat meat—*once a day* if obliged to fast, and *several times a day* if not obliged to fast—
   a) On Ember Days;
   b) On Wednesdays of Lent—except Ash Wednesday and Wednesday of Holy Week;
   c) On Vigils of Pentecost, Assumption, All Saints'.

III. *Those obliged to fast* may eat meat *once a day* on the other days of Lent.

IV. *Those not obliged to fast* may eat meat several times a day on the other days of Lent.

V. *There is no fast or abstinence* on Sundays, or on Holy-Days of Obligation, unless such a Holy-Day falls in Lent.

VI. *The Lenten season ends* at noon on Holy Saturday. Those obliged to fast may not eat meat before noon on account of the obligation of the fast.

8. *Paul,* a bank clerk, got a dispensation from fasting during Lent. On days when flesh meat was allowed to fasters at the principal meal, Paul took meat two or three times a day. Was he justified in doing so? On a Friday he accepted an invitation to dinner given by the Automobile Club of his city, and he did not abstain. He thought he was allowed to eat what was served on such occasions. Did he do wrong?

9. Has the State the right to *control* the manufacture and sale of intoxicating beverages? Has it the right to *forbid* the moderate use of such beverages? Is prohibition a cure for the drink evil? Can you suggest a better remedy?

10. What is the purpose of dress? Why is immodesty in dress such a great evil?

11. Write a paragraph on "the use and abuse of recreation and amusement."

12. What is *Suicide?* What motives for suicide recur most frequently?

13. Why is direct and deliberate suicide always a mortal sin?

14. Does the Church deny Christian burial to all suicides?

15. When would you be permitted to risk your life? What about Dueling?

16. Is it allowed to desire death?

17. Why does the Church forbid Cremation? How was cremation introduced in modern times? Would it ever be allowed to burn the dead? Would the beautiful prayers and ceremonies of the Church at funerals have any meaning if cremation were adopted?

3. CHASTITY AND ITS VIOLATION

1. What is the purpose of the sexual powers bestowed on us by God? What commandment forbids us to abuse or misuse them?

2. When is celibacy or virginity more pleasing to God than marriage?
3. Read John 2,1-12. What does this incident tell us about Christ's attitude towards marriage?
4. What do we understand by the virtue of *Chastity*? Why is it so called?
5. Does Chastity demand control only of external acts against purity? What does Christ demand? See Matt. 5,27-28.
6. Show that Chastity is a most beautiful virtue, productive of the greatest benefits to man.
7. What sins are forbidden by the Sixth and Ninth Commandments?
8. Is every sin against purity grievous? When does an impure thought or imagination become sinful?
9. Are all sins of impurity of equal malice? Explain.
10. "Impurity desecrates our human dignity." Comment on these words.
11. What does St. Paul say about sins of impurity?
12. Show that impurity is a sin against human society.
13. What means, natural and supernatural, must we use to preserve the virtue of chastity? Illustrate your answer by examples from Scripture and the Lives of the Saints.
14. *Reading*: Joseph J. Williams, S.J., *Keep the Gate.*

    St. John the Evangelist, the Virgin Apostle.—"How beautiful and majestic is the image of that great Apostle, Evangelist and Prophet of the Church, who came so early into Our Lord's chosen company, and lived so long after all his fellows. We can contemplate him in his youth and in his venerable age; and on his whole life, from first to last, as his special gift, is marked *purity*. He is the Virgin Apostle, who on that account was so dear to his Lord, 'the disciple whom Jesus loved,' who lay on His Bosom, who received His Mother from Him when upon the Cross, who had the vision of all the wonders which were to come to pass in the world to the end of time. 'Greatly to be honored,' says the Church, 'is blessed John, who on the Lord's Breast lay at supper, to whom, a virgin, did Christ on the Cross commit His Virgin Mother. He was chosen a virgin by the Lord, and was more beloved than the rest. The special prerogative of chastity had made him meet for his Lord's larger love, because, being chosen by Him a virgin, a virgin he remained unto the end.' He it was who in his youth professed his readiness to drink Christ's chalice with Him; who wore away a long life as a desolate stranger in a foreign land; who was at length carried to Rome and plunged into the hot oil, and then was banished to a far island, till his days drew near their close" (CARDINAL NEWMAN).

4. DUTIES CONCERNING MATERIAL GOODS

1. What do we mean by the Right of Private Property?
2. Show that the right of private ownership rests on the divine law.
3. Show that private ownership is necessary, taking man as he is, for the welfare of the individual and of society.
4. What has always been the attitude of the Church on the question of private property?

DUTIES TOWARDS OURSELVES

5. What does Pope Leo XIII teach about the origin of private property?
6. What was Christ's attitude towards material goods? Does He forbid us to seek after them? Why does He warn us against striving after wealth?
7. "We are only *stewards* of what we possess." Comment on these words.
8. Read the parables of the Rich Man and Lazarus (Luke 16,19-31) and of the Wealthy Farmer (Luke 12,16-21). What lessons do they teach?
9. Distinguish between *Communism* and *Socialism*.
10. Read *Acts* 2,44-45. How does the communism of the first Christians differ from the communism forced on the Russian people to-day?
11. Why is Socialism unjust and impracticable?
12. What is capitalism? When does it become a menace to society?
13. Show that the Gospel of Christ is the only true solution of the Social question.
14. *Readings:*
     a) *Question Box,* pp. 417-418: "Private Property," and pp. 414-415: "Communism in the Early Church."
     b) Pope Pius XI, Encyclical *Quadragesimo Anno,* On Reconstructing the Social Order and Perfecting it Conformably to the Precepts of the Gospel.
     Catholic and Socialist Are Contradictory Terms.—"If, like all errors, socialism contains a certain element of truth (and this the Sovereign Pontiffs have never denied), it is nevertheless founded upon a doctrine of human society peculiarly its own, which is opposed to true Christianity. 'Religious Socialism,' 'Christian Socialism' are expressions implying a contradiction in terms. No one can be at the same time a sincere Catholic and a true socialist" (Pius XI, Encyclical *Quadragesimo Anno*).

THE IMPIETY OF CAPITAL AND LABOR

The impiety of capital, which would treat the workman like a machine, must be broken. It is a crime against the working classes; it degrades them. It fits in with the theory of those who would trace man's descent to the ape.

But the impiety of labor must also be guarded against. If the movement in favor of higher wages oversteps the bounds of justice, catastrophes must necessarily ensue, the whole weight of which will recoil on the working-classes. But if the working-classes are to observe just moderation in their demands, if they are to escape the danger of becoming mere tools in the hands of ambitious and unscrupulous demagogues, if they wish to keep clear of the inordinate selfishness which they condemn so severely in the capitalist, they must be filled with a lofty moral sense, their ranks must be made up of courageous, Christian, religious men. The power of money without religion is an evil, but the power of organized labor without religion is just as great an evil. Both lead to destruction.—METLAKE, *Ketteler and the Christian Social Reform Movement* (Philadelphia: The Dolphin Press), p. 163.

CHAPTER III

Our Duties Towards Our Neighbor

Man is born to live with his kind; in other words, man is by nature a *social being*. Hence he has the obligation not merely to respect the rights of his fellow-men, but also to give them whatever assistance they may require. *Justice* and *charity* are the foundations of human society.

Our holy Faith teaches us to regard all men without exception as *images of God* with whom we share the same origin and the same destiny. The duties of justice and charity thus receive a supernatural motivation and a universality unknown to pre-Christian times. By placing charity above justice, without setting aside the claims of justice, the Gospel gives to social life a leaven which enables the individual to rise to the highest efforts for the common good, and raises society itself to a state of perfection and fruitfulness undreamed of before the coming of Christ.

I. NATURE AND PROPERTIES OF CHRISTIAN CHARITY

1. In the teaching of Christ the love of God and the love of our neighbor stand on the same plane.—"The second is like unto this: Thou shalt love thy neighbor as thyself." Christ makes the love of our neighbor the mark by which His disciples are known: "By this shall all men know that you are My disciples, if you have love for one another" (John 13,35). There is an intimate and necessary relationship between the love of God and the love of our neighbor; the love of our neighbor is the choice fruit, and the measure as well, of our love of God: "If any man say, I love God, and hateth his brother, he is a liar. For he that loveth not his brother, whom he seeth, how can he love God, whom he seeth not. And this commandment we have from God, that he who loveth God, love also his brother" (1 John 4,20-21).

2. Our Lord calls the commandment of love a new commandment, although we find it formulated in the Book of Leviticus (19,18). It was in fact a new commandment. It was unknown to the pagan world, and falsely interpreted by the Jews, who excluded all non-Jews from their love. In the Parable of the Good Samaritan the hated foreigner and national foe has to teach the priest and the levite who is their neighbor.

3. Christian charity is something more than natural sympathy.—It is based on the recognition of the *value of our neighbor's soul,* on reverence and esteem for the image of God impressed on that soul. Purely human affection retains at bottom a certain amount of selfishness. The charity demanded by Christ must be independent of flesh and blood. Only such love can go out to the poorest and the most degraded, because they too are children of God. "If you love them that love you, what reward shall you have? Do not even the publicans this? And if you salute your brethren only, what do you more? Do not also the heathens this? Be you therefore perfect, as also your heavenly Father is perfect" (Matt. 5,46).

4. Christian charity is a necessary part of the Christian religion.—Just as the life of Christ was loving service to all, so true Christian piety and true imitation of Christ can only be found where the same spirit of universal love is found. "I have given you an example, that as I have done to you, so you do also" (John 13,15).

5. Qualities of Christian Charity.—From the nature of charity we can readily see what qualities it possesses:

a) It is a sincere *disposition of the heart,* not a matter of feeling. Hence it can be the object of a command. Love founded on feeling only cannot be commanded.

b) It is *unselfish* according to the words of the Apostle: "Charity is not ambitious, seeketh not her own" (1 Cor. 13,5).

c) It is *universal,* embracing all men without exception, independent of all economical, social, and national differences.

d) It is *active,* ever ready to help others who are in need.

"See how they love one another," the pagans cried out in astonishment when they beheld the effects of true charity manifested by the early Christians, and this charity won innumerable friends and adherents for the new religion.

2. Well-Ordered Charity

1. The Virtue of Charity Must Be Regulated by Prudence and Temperance.—For charity does not consist in blind service

CHRIST WASHES THE FEET OF THE APOSTLES
"I have given you an example." (John 13, 15)

Tintoretto

of our neighbor, but in service that keeps in view the ends to be attained. True charity cannot indeed be fenced about and hedged in; but there are limits which it is bound to respect.

2. **"Charity Begins at Home."**—Our Lord laid down the so-called *Golden Rule*: "All things whatsoever ye would that men should do to you, do you also to them, for this is the law and the prophets" (Matt. 7,12). Similar to this is the proverb: "Charity begins at home." That does not mean that we should think of ourselves first and then only of others. It really means that there are certain goods, such as our eternal salvation, which we cannot surrender or endanger under any circumstances. In other words, we must never exercise charity towards our neighbor in such a manner as to neglect our own duties.

3. **Rules of Charity.**—If we look at the *objects or goods* to which our charity can be directed, two general rules may be laid down:

a) We must be ready to sacrifice every temporal good for the salvation of our neighbor's soul. "In this we have known the charity of God, because He hath laid down His life for us, and *we ought to lay down our lives for the brethren*" (1 John 3,16).

Such an obligation is, of course, very rare. As a rule we do our duty to our neighbor in this respect if we pray for his spiritual welfare, give him good example, and prevent him from committing sin when we can. We are certainly guilty of sin, if our neighbor's spiritual welfare is a matter of complete indifference to us.

b) The greater our neighbor's need is, the greater personal sacrifices we are obliged to make for him. Christ Himself enforces this duty under the threat of eternal reprobation (Matt. 25,11).

When our neighbor lacks that which is indispensable for the preservation of life, we are obliged to assist him not only from our abundance, but even from that which is necessary for the suitable maintenance of our state; for well-ordered charity requires that we prefer the life of our neighbor as a good of a higher order to that comfort which our station in life may claim. When our neighbor is in any need whatever we are obliged to assist him at least from our abundance. St. Paul says to Timothy: "Charge the rich of this world to do good, to be rich in good works, to *give easily*, to communicate to others" (1 Tim. 6,17).

In regard to the *persons* towards whom our charity is to be exercised, we must help those first who are nearest to us by ties of blood and religion, of love and friendship, of home and country.

Hence parents must help their own children first, children their parents, Christians their fellow-Christians, etc. St. Paul himself makes this latter distinction when he says: "Let us work good to all men, but especially to those who are of the household of the faith" (Gal. 6,10).

3. CORPORAL AND SPIRITUAL WORKS OF MERCY

The duty of relieving the temporal and spiritual needs of our neighbor is performed in diverse ways, but chiefly by the so-called *corporal* and *spiritual works of mercy*.

1. Our Lord mentions six corporal works of mercy: feeding the hungry, giving drink to the thirsty, clothing the naked, harboring strangers, visiting the sick, visiting prisoners (Matt. 25,41-43). A seventh: burying the dead, was added from Tob. 12,22. The following hexameter will assist the memory of the Latin scholar:

Visito, poto, cibo, redimo, tego, colligo, condo.

Of each of these works of mercy Christ says: "As long as you did it to one of these My least brethren, you did it to Me." What greater or more forcible motive to charity can we have than the assurance that the Son of God will accept all good offices done to the afflicted as done to Himself?

2. There are also seven ways of relieving the wants of our neighbor's soul: to convert the sinner, to instruct the ignorant, to counsel the doubtful, to comfort the sorrowful, to bear wrongs patiently, to forgive injuries, to pray for the living and the dead.

Consule, carpe, doce, solare, remitte, fer, ora.

These works of mercy cover all the spiritual needs and ills with which mankind is afflicted. Most of us have an opportunity of practicing them daily; and we will practice them the more zealously, the more vividly we realize the value of a single soul in the eyes of God.

3. Amongst the corporal works of mercy **Almsgiving,** or the timely assisting of one in need, takes the first place. Four of the seven works are devoted to it. Numerous passages in the Old and New Testaments admonish us to practice it and extol its value in the sight of God. Christ makes God's mercy towards us dependent

A Corporal Work of Mercy
St. Pantaleon, a Physician of the Third Century, Visiting the Sick

on our mercy towards our fellow-men. He tells us to make unto ourselves friends with the riches of this world, and to collect imperishable treasures which the rust and the moth cannot consume, nor the thief steal. St. John the Baptist taught the people that whatever they had more than their own wants required should be bestowed upon their needy brethren (Luke 3,11).

The Fathers of the Church went even further than Christ and His Apostles in their demands. St. Augustine wants the rich to give *all their abundance to the poor. Superflua divitum necessaria sunt pauperum. Res alienae possidentur, cum superflua possidentur.*

4. It is impossible to express in figures just **what percentage of our wealth we are obliged to give to the poor.** The well-to-do must remember that they have not fulfilled the law of

Schäufelin

A CORPORAL WORK OF MERCY
Feeding the Hungry

almsgiving by paying the taxes from which the expenses of public charity are defrayed. Every Catholic should belong to some charitable religious society, such as the St. Vincent de Paul Conference.

But it is not enough to give food, drink, clothing, and shelter to the needy; our charity must be free from vainglory and be seasoned with genuine love and sympathy and kindliness: without this our alms-deeds are worth nothing before God and may do more harm than good to those whom we succor.

5. Amongst the spiritual works of mercy a conspicuous place is assigned by Our Lord to **Fraternal Correction.** It consists in admonishing our neighbor of his faults or of his sins *through a motive of charity.* "If thy brother shall offend against thee, go and rebuke him between thee and him alone. If he shall hear thee, thou shalt gain thy brother" (Matt. 18,15).

Superiors are bound to practice fraternal correction towards their subjects at all times; others only when it is likely to profit their neighbor. It should therefore be omitted when the contrary effect is likely to ensue. It must always be administered with all possible prudence and humility. Everyone has his failings and stands in need of indulgence from others: "Brethren, if a man be overtaken in any fault, you who are spiritual instruct such a one in the spirit of mildness, considering thyself, lest thou also be tempted" (Gal. 6,1). St. James tells us the reward of successful fraternal correction: "He who causeth a sinner to be converted from the error of his way shall save his soul from death, and shall cover a multitude of sins" (James 5,20).

4. Love Your Enemies

1. In the universality of our charity our enemies, too, must be included.—Against the pharisaical interpretation of the law of charity Christ emphatically insisted on charity towards our enemies: "You have heard that it hath been said, Thou shalt love thy neighbor, and hate thy enemy. But I say to you, *Love your enemies,* do good to them that hate you, and pray for them that persecute and calumniate you" (Matt. 5,43-44).

The words "hate thy enemy" are not found in the Old Testament; they were added by the Scribes and Pharisees. In the writings of the pagan philosophers we find an occasional allusion to the necessity of loving our

THE DIVINE VICTIM ON CALVARY
"Father, forgive them . . ." (Luke 23, 34)

enemies; but both Jews and pagans looked upon it as something extraordinary, an exception which could not be made a rule. Since the Sermon on the Mount it is part and parcel of the Christian life, the fruit of true charity by which the Christian becomes like his Heavenly Father.

2. In order to fulfill our Lord's command to love our enemies, it is not sufficient to abstain from revenging ourselves on those who have injured us; we must acknowledge their good qualities, wish them well, pray for them, and be ready to assist them in their needs; we must forgive them from our hearts, and even return good for evil. The love of our enemies does not, however, compel us to give up our just rights.

3. Christ is the most perfect model of love for enemies.— He practiced it in a sublime degree in His life and at the hour of His death. "Father, forgive them, for they know not what they do."

"Then came Peter unto Him and said: Lord, how often shall my brother offend against me, and I forgive him? Till seven times? Jesus saith to him: I say not to thee, till seven times; but till seventy times seven times" (Matt. 18,21-22).

"To no man render evil for evil. . . . Do not revenge yourselves, my dearly beloved, but give place unto wrath, for it is written: Revenge is Mine; I will repay, saith the Lord. But if thy enemy be hungry, give him to eat, if he thirst, give him to drink; for, doing this, thou shalt heap coals of fire upon his head. Be not overcome by evil, but overcome evil by good" (Rom. 12,17-21).

The Emperor Marcus Aurelius, conversing on a certain occasion with one of his officers about those who professed the Christian faith, characterized them as fools. The officer assented, adding: "They even pray for their executioners." "If that is so, I reverse my judgment," said the Emperor, "their religion must be holy and divine."

5. Violations of Charity

1. The Sin of Hatred.—Directly opposed to the love of our neighbor is *hatred* of him. Hatred is more than want of love. It separates us interiorly from our neighbor. It not only forgets every duty toward him, but positively desires to injure him.

When directed against the *person* of our neighbor, hatred is always grievously sinful. If it is directed against the *bad qualities* of our neighbor, it may be without sin, for bad qualities are really hateful. But this kind of hatred usually passes from the bad qualities to the person of our neighbor, and is therefore sinful.

Hatred grieves at the prosperity and rejoices at the adversity of the hated person; it exaggerates his faults and discounts his virtues; it wishes evil and does evil to him; it does not stop at malediction, calumny and detraction, but often assails his very life. Hence Holy Scripture says: "Whosoever hateth his brother is a murderer."

2. In the train of hatred we always find revenge.—It is the deliberate infliction of injury, or the desire of so doing, in return for an injury received. Holy Scripture warns us to leave the punishment of those who injure us to God: "Say not: I will return evil; wait for the Lord, and He will deliver thee" (Prov. 20,22).

3. Envy is a feeling of sadness aroused at the sight of another's superiority or success, whether in the spiritual or the temporal order. It leads to rash judgment, calumny, and detraction. It is essentially selfishness, and finds delight in destroying the joys and pleasures of others.

> "Base envy withers at another's joy,
> And hates that excellence it cannot reach."

Through the envy of the devil, says the Book of Wisdom, sin came into the world, by which the bliss of Paradise was lost. The ugliest form of envy is displeasure and discontent at another's spiritual progress. *It is one of the sins against the Holy Ghost.*

4. Scandal, which literally means "the spring of a trap," includes whatever may be to our neighbor the occasion of his spiritual downfall. It may be *direct*, i.e., foreseen and intended; or *indirect*, i.e., foreseen, but not intended.

There is a twofold malice in sins of direct scandal; such sins are against charity and also against the special virtue which he who suffers scandal violates. So that, when A excites B to drink to excess, A sins against charity and against temperance (Slater, *Moral Theology*).

In the case of indirect scandal the sin may arise from the malice of our neighbor who makes evil out of what is harmless—*pharisaical scandal*; or from his ignorance and weakness—*scandal of the weak.*

We must never neglect to do our duty because the ill-disposed choose to be scandalized at our conduct; but we must try to prevent scandalizing the weak, especially children, either by enlightening their ignorance or by altogether avoiding the action which causes them to be scandalized. "Wherefore if meat scandalize my brother, I will never eat flesh, lest I should scandalize my brother" (1 Cor. 8,13).

5. Direct scandal is an evil condemned by Christ in the severest terms.—"He that shall scandalize one of these little ones that believe in Me, it were better for him that a millstone should be hanged about his neck, and that he should be drowned in the depth of the sea" (Matt. 18,6). The seducer to sin destroys the spiritual life of his neighbor's soul and drags him down into his own rebellion against God. "Be brothers of the Angels, and Angels of your brothers," says St. Bernard. The seducer acts the part of the devil towards his brothers.

6. Co-operating with the Sins of Others.—Direct scandal, or seduction to sin, must be distinguished from *co-operation with the sins of others*. Direct scandal calls forth the sin, whereas co-operation consists in assisting another to commit a sin which he is already determined to commit. Co-operation is called *formal* when it embraces the sin itself; otherwise it is *material* only.

Formal co-operation is always wrong, because it is a direct participation in another's sin; material co-operation, which stands only distantly in relationship with another's sin, may be permitted under the following conditions:

a) The act must be in itself good or at least indifferent;

b) There must be a grave reason for performing the act;

c) The sin of the other must be neither desired nor consented to.

6. THOU SHALT NOT KILL

We must love our neighbor as ourselves. Consequently, just as we must have a well-ordered solicitude for our own life and health, so we must also respect and safeguard the life and health of our neighbor.

1. We injure our neighbor's health by inflicting severe pain or bodily injury on him; by quarreling with him, exciting him to anger, or in other ways depriving him of interior peace and content; by adulterating articles of food; by playing dangerous practical jokes on him (hazing and initiation); by culpable negligence, such as reckless driving, carelessness in handling dangerous weapons; by forcing him to overexert himself, or to live and work in unsanitary surroundings; by refusing to give him a living wage, when we are able to do so; by compelling women or children to do work unsuited to their age or sex . . .

2. Murder.—The most heinous crime against our neighbor's life is *murder*, one of the four sins crying to Heaven for vengeance. God said to Cain: "What hast thou done? The voice of thy brother's blood crieth to Me from the earth" (Gen. 4,10). The murderer commits an outrage against the rights of God as the author and preserver of human life, against the highest and most valuable temporal good of his neighbor, and against the safety of human society at large.

Parents, nurses, doctors, and others who, through malice or negligence, bring about the death of a child before or after its birth, are guilty of murder.

But the putting to death of another is not always a sin. *Soldiers* fighting in a just war do not sin by taking the life of the enemy.

Marillier

"What has thou done? The voice of thy brother's, blood crieth to Me from the earth." (Gen. 4, 10)

But the desire and intention of the soldier should not be primarily to kill, but only to put the enemy beyond the possibility of doing further harm. Death will be the result of his efforts in many cases, and this he permits to occur rather than desires and intends. He has no right to slay outside of battle or without the express command of a superior officer; if he does so, he is guilty of murder.

3. Capital punishment inflicted by the state after the conviction of a criminal, is not murder. In the Old Testament God Himself delegated His supreme right over life to His creatures: "Whoever sheds human blood, let his blood be shed." In the New Testament the officer of the law is called by St. Paul the minister of God and is said not without cause to carry the sword; and the sword is the symbol of the power to inflict death.

4. He does not commit a sin who kills another in self-defense.—I may repel an unjust aggressor, i.e., anyone who has no right to threaten my life, even at the cost of his life under certain conditions.

These conditions are:

a) That I use no greater violence than is necessary to ward off danger to my own life;

b) That I inflict violence on the aggressor *during* the very act of aggression; neither before nor after;

c) That I have no other means, such as flight or calling for help, of avoiding the danger;

d) That I do not directly intend the death of the aggressor, but only the defense of my own life.

5. But has one a right to kill in defense of other goods besides life?—If there be no other means of defending material goods of great importance, their possessor has the right to take the life of the robber who attempts to deprive him of them or to retain them.

For unjust attack upon one's reputation or good name, the right of self-defense obviously does not extend so far as the taking of the calumniator's life. There are other and more effectual means of redress.

A woman has the right to defend her virtue by taking the life, if need be, of the aggressor. One who threatens a woman's honor not only violates her right to personal integrity, but also her right of natural independence.

6. The killing of animals is not murder, as some fanatics claim. Animals have no rights because they are not intelligent and free. If they had rights, they would also have duties; but no one will say that they have duties. But to deny that animals have rights is certainly not saying that we may treat them according as our fancy moves us. God made them and has rights in them, so we have a duty to God not to misuse them (Vaughan, *Thoughts for All Times*, p. 382).

7. Thou Shalt Not Steal

1. I have the right to acquire and possess private property; my neighbor has the same right; hence it is my duty to respect his right, just as it is his duty to respect mine. This duty is violated by *Theft, Robbery, Fraud,* and *Usury;* by injuring another's property, by detaining goods that have been found or lent, and by the non-payment of debts.

2. Theft consists in taking what belongs to another secretly and contrary to the rational will of the owner. To steal when starving, or as the only means of saving one's life in an extremity, is not a sin, provided one has the intention of restoring, if possible, what one has stolen.

To conceal or purchase goods that are known to have been stolen, is as bad as theft. It is also theft to do less work than we ought, and yet to exact full payment. Small thefts are grievously sinful, if the thief has the intention of repeating them and thereby reaching a considerable sum, because each of these thefts is committed with a gravely bad intention.

3. Robbery consists in taking what belongs to another either openly or by violence. An employer who should refuse to pay his employees their just wages would be guilty of robbery; indeed such a man would commit a sin crying to Heaven for vengeance. "Behold the hire of the laborers, which by fraud has been kept back by you, crieth; and the cry of them hath entered into the ears of the Lord of Sabaoth" (James 5,4).

4. Fraud or cheating consists in injuring our neighbor in his possession by crafty means, e.g., by using false weights and measures; by supplying goods inferior to what has been agreed upon; by issuing or passing counterfeit money—the fact that we have been deceived does not give us the right to deceive others; by falsifying documents; by asking too much for our wares, or by concealing from the purchaser a notable defect in them; by fraud-

ulently declaring bankruptcy; by giving and taking bribes. "Let
no man overreach or circumvent his brother in business" (1 Thess.
4,6).

5. Usury is a species of fraud, and consists in exacting for
the loan of money more interest than the general practice and the
laws of the country allow. A *speculator* who buys up food and
keeps it until a time of scarcity in order to sell it at a higher price,
is really a usurer.

The taking of interest was forbidden in the Old Testament; the Church
retained the prohibition for many centuries. When under the modern
economical system it became evident that commerce could not exist without
a rate of interest, the prohibition was removed.

6. We may injure our neighbor's property, if we set it on
fire, if we damage his goods, tread down his crops, fish or shoot
on his grounds without permission. If we do this willfully and
with malice, it is certainly grievously sinful.

**7. All injury to our neighbor's goods is more or less sinful
according to the harm done.**—Taking a small sum would, as a
rule, not constitute a mortal sin; but to take it from a poor person
would be a very grave matter, if the thief knew that it would
cause him serious injury.

8. Restitution.—When any act of injustice has been committed,
it is not enough to repent in order to obtain pardon; *restitution* is
also necessary; that is, we must give back the ill-gotten goods and,
as far as in us lies, repair the injury we have done. "The sin is
not forgiven," says St. Augustine, "unless the stolen goods be
restored, if they can be restored." If we can not do this at once,
we must have the intention of doing so as soon as possible.

The obligation of restitution, which can be canceled only by
the person wronged, rests in the first place on him who did the
wrong; then on all who took part in it; lastly on those who, being
obliged in justice to prevent it, failed to do so.

If the owner or his heirs are dead or cannot be found, the
ill-gotten goods or their equivalent must be given to the poor or
devoted to religious purposes.

If I possess another's property in *good faith*, that is, if I do not
know that it belonged to another, I am bound to restore it as soon
as I advert to the fact, but I have the right to deduct all expenses
I incurred while it was in my possession.

If I injured my neighbor's property without my will and knowledge, I am obliged to make restitution only in case a court of justice condemns me to do so.

8. THE DUTY OF TRUTHFULNESS AND FIDELITY

1. The Virtue of Truthfulness consists in the constant endeavor to make our words harmonize with our thoughts and feelings. *Fidelity* is the readiness to keep one's promises. Both of these virtues are of fundamental importance for the welfare of society. We sin against truthfulness by *lying* and *hypocrisy*; against fidelity, by *breaking our promises or our given word*

2. A Lie consists in affirming as true what we know to be false, or in denying as true what we know to be true. If we assert something as true, firmly believing it to be true, while as a fact it is false; or if we sincerely affirm something as false, while in reality it is true,—such statements are not *lies*: they are simply *errors*.

3. There are three kinds of lies.—(*a*) the *jocose lie*, or the lie told in jest; (*b*) the *officious lie*, which is told to ward off some evil or to procure some advantage for ourselves or our neighbor; (*c*) the *malicious lie*, which is told with the intention of injuring another.

A lie is wrong not merely because it may do harm to another person, but because it violates the moral order, and because it is essentially opposed to God, who is truth itself, and to the end for which speech was given to man.

Hence every deliberate lie is a sin.—The jocose and the officious lie never exceed a venial sin when they do no injury to anyone, or cause no grave scandal. When words contrary to truth are said in jest there is no lie at all if the untruth is quite evident. A *malicious lie* is a mortal sin whenever it causes a serious injury to our neighbor's goods or honor.

4. Hypocrisy and dissimulation, or hiding under false appearances,—"wolves in sheep's clothing,"—are lies in action, and no less to be condemned than lies in word.

5. Mental Reservation is a means of concealing a truth which we have no right to divulge or which the inquirer has no right to know. It consists in using words in a sense other than that which is obvious, with the intention of letting the inquirer deceive himself. It is also called *equivocation*. If I tell a beggar that I have

Ponce

ANANIAS AND SAPHIRA

no money in my pocket, meaning that I have no money for him, I am using mental reservation; I am inserting *mentally* something which I do not express.

If the reservation or equivocation is of such a nature that it cannot be perceived by the hearer, then the person using it certainly sins. On the other hand, it is lawful to use a mental reservation which *may be*, though very likely *will not be*, understood from the circumstances. Thus a priest is perfectly justified in denying that he knows a crime which he has only learnt through sacramental confession.

It must be remembered, however, that a just cause is needed to make mental reservation lawful; that it is sinful when a man is put under oath by just authority; that it must not be used in making contracts, or generally in matters concerning the interests of others. "A *habit* of equivocation is detestable to all good men, and the practice of perfect simplicity and straightforwardness is not only estimable and engaging and virtuous, but it is also the wisest course." Abhorrence of lies in every shape and form is the test of character. (The whole question of lying and equivocation is treated by Cardinal Newman in his *Apologia*, Note G.)

6. Fidelity has been well called the "twin-sister of truthfulness." Truthfulness consists in the harmony between our thoughts and our words; fidelity is the harmony between our acts and our given word. Fidelity is the surest foundation of every relation of man to man. "It is the ruler's second crown, the official's daily oath of office, the workman's best tool, the servant's most valuable recommendation, the inexhaustible source of blessing to the family, the most glorious epitaphs of the dead" (Cardinal Faulhaber).

9. OUR NEIGHBOR'S REPUTATION

1. Honor and good name are more valuable than material goods. Hence the law of charity obliges us to respect and protect our neighbor's good name as carefully as our own.

> Mine honor is my life; both grow in one;
> Take honor from me, and my life is done.
> —SHAKESPEARE.

2. We violate this duty in thought by *false suspicion*, when without reason or just cause, we surmise evil of our neighbor; and by *rash judgment*, when, without sufficient reason, we believe the evil to be true. "Charity thinketh no evil." "Judge not and you shall not be judged."

3. We violate this duty in words by *contumely, detraction, calumny* and *tale-bearing*.

a) **Contumely** is more than speaking of a person's known faults before his face. Its object is to prevent your good name from getting the respect it deserves by offering just the contrary; by expression of contempt offered to your face; by calling opprobrious names, flinging vile epithets, making shameful charges; by scorn, ridicule, indecent mockery and caricature that cover you with shame and confusion.

b) **Detraction** is injury done to our neighbor's good name by making known without just cause some fault or crime of which he is really guilty, or is believed to be guilty.

c) **Calumny** or slander is a false charge or imputation against our neighbor's good name. It is a graver sin than detraction, for it is opposed not only to justice but also to truth.

If it is wrong to take away our neighbor's character by calumny or detraction, it is also wrong to take pleasure in listening to the evil which is asserted of him. "The one has the devil on his tongue, the other in his ear," says St. Bernard.

As both detraction and calumny are sins against justice they involve the obligation of restitution as far as possible for the unjust damage which they cause.

d) **Tale-bearing,** called "whispering" in the Bible, consists in repeating to a person the unfavorable things that another has said of him. It is a detestable sin. There is no surer way of destroying the peace and harmony of friends and families than that of tale-bearing. "The whisperer and the double-tongued is accursed; for he hath troubled many that were at peace. The tale-bearer shall defile his own soul, and shall be hated by all. Hast thou heard a word against thy neighbor? Let it die within thee, trusting that it will not burst thee" (Ecclus. 19,10; 21-31; 28,15).

SUGGESTIONS FOR STUDY AND REVIEW

1. Why are Justice and Charity the foundations of human society?
2. The Gospel places Charity above Justice. Of what significance is this for the individual and for society?

1. NATURE AND PROPERTIES OF CHRISTIAN CHARITY

1. Show that Christ places love of God and love of our neighbor on the same plane.
2. Read the parable of the Good Samaritan (Luke 10,30-37). What did Our Lord wish to teach by it? What Jewish and pagan conception of charity did He combat?
3. Show that Christian charity is more than natural sympathy or purely human affection.
4. Why is Christian charity a necessary part of the Christian Religion?
5. What qualities must our charity have? Find examples to illustrate your answers.
6. *Practice Charity.*—"The real love of man *must* depend on practice, and therefore must begin by exercising itself on our friends around us, otherwise it will have no existence. By trying to love our relations and friends, by submitting to their wishes, though contrary to our own, by bearing with their infirmities, by overcoming their occasional waywardness by kindness, by dwelling on their excellences, and trying to copy them, thus it is that we form in our hearts that root of charity, which, though small at first, may like the mustard seed, at last even overshadow the earth" (NEWMAN).

2. WELL-ORDERED CHARITY

1. Why must Charity be regulated by Prudence and Temperance?

2. "Charity begins at home." Explain this proverb. (What does it not mean? What does it mean?)
3. What rules must guide us in the exercise of our charity?
4. *James*, a Catholic day-laborer, and father of a family, has been out of work for several months. The rent for his house is in arrears, and the landlord has given him notice to move out unless the rent is paid by the end of the week. In his necessity James goes to *Martin*, a well-to-do Catholic, and asks him for help towards paying his rent; neighbors, he tells him, are helping him to feed his family. Martin refuses to assist him, telling him to apply to the local branch of the Salvation Army. Was Martin under grave obligation to help his poor fellow-Catholic? (See Gal. 6,10). What would Our Lord say to Martin's conduct? (See Matt. 25,42).
5. *What Makes Friendship Lasting?*—"No one really loves another who does not feel a certain reverence towards him. When friends transgress this sobriety of affection, they may indeed continue to associate for a time, but they have broken the bond of union. It is *mutual respect* which makes friendship lasting" (NEWMAN).

3. CORPORAL AND SPIRITUAL WORKS OF MERCY

1. Name the corporal works of mercy. How many of these are mentioned by Our Lord?
2. What does Christ say of each of these works of mercy? From what motive should we practice them?
3. How can we relieve the wants of our neighbor's soul?
4. Write a paper on *Almsgiving*, using the following hints:
    1) What is Almsgiving?
    2) Its place among the Corporal Works of Mercy.
    3) Almsgiving recommended in the Scriptures: Heb. 13,16; Gal. 5,13; Luke 12,33; 16,9; 3,11.
    4) How we should give alms: Matt. 6,2-4; 2 Cor. 9,7.
    5) Value of Almsgiving in the sight of God: Matt. 10,42; Heb. 6,10.
    6) Examples of Almsgiving: Tobias 1,19; Acts 9,36; Luke 19,8-9.
    7) The Sin and Punishment of Selfishness: James 2,15-16; Luke 16,19.
5. In what does Fraternal Correction consist? Is there an obligation to give fraternal correction?
6. By whom is fraternal correction to be given, to whom, and in what way?
7. Examples of loving reproof: Our Lord, Matt. 16,23; St. Peter, Acts 5,3; St. John the Baptist, Mark 6,18; St. Paul, Acts 23,3; the Good Thief, Luke 23,40.
8. Faulty modes of correction: Matt. 7,3-5.
9. *Almsgiving a Strict Obligation.*—"People are only too often disposed to look upon almsgiving as a good work indeed, but not as a strict obligation. Such a conception is a fundamental error in a Christian soul. I maintain, on the contrary, with St. Thomas and St. Alphonsus, that almsgiving in general is a strict obligation the fulfillment of which is necessary for salvation.

"The obligation of almsgiving can be realized by an appeal to con-

science only, not by coercion. He who breaks a law binding in justice is
a thief, or a defrauder, or a robber; he who violates the law of charity
is no less a sinner; for the precept of charity occupies a higher place in
the eyes of God than the precept of justice. Not the spirit of God but the
spirit of the world has taught the world to put a false value on these
actions. For while the world despises and abhors theft, and justly so,
while it connects the idea of shame with theft, and rightly so, hard-
heartedness, uncharitableness, avarice are not generally held in the odor
of disgrace, and in this the world is altogether wrong. It will not be thus
on the Day of Judgment. . . ."—BISHOP KETTELER: *Ketteler and the
Christian Social Reform Movement*, by GEORGE METLAKE (Philadelphia:
The Dolphin Press, pp. 63-64).

4. LOVE YOUR ENEMIES

1. Show that Christian charity includes love of enemies.
2. In what does love of our enemies consist? Give examples.
3. Show how Christ taught us by word and example to love our enemies.
4. How did the first martyr, St. Stephen, imitate Our Lord? Find other
   examples.
5. Read the parable of the Unmerciful Servant, Matt. 18,23-35. What lesson
   should we learn from it? In what prayer is this lesson contained?
6. When tempted to hate those who seek to injure you, say to yourself:
   "Thy enemy is a creature of God, made in His image. We honor the
   effigy of the ruler, whether it be stamped in gold or copper; in the same
   way we must reverence God's image whether it be contemplated in a
   good or evil man. Hate the faults which are the work of evil men,
   but love the man who is the work of God. Bethink thee that the
   wicked are instruments in the hand of God, as the leech in the hand of
   the physician" (PESCH).

5. VIOLATIONS OF CHARITY

1. Describe a person who is actuated (a) by hatred, (b) by envy, (c) by
   revenge.
2. What is meant by Scandal?
3. Distinguish between direct and indirect scandal. Give an example of each.
4. When is one obliged to avoid giving indirect scandal?
5. Quote Our Lord's condemnation of scandal-givers.
6. What is co-operation in another's sin, and how far is it lawful?
7. *Mary*, a Catholic, and *Martha*, an Episcopalian, often help each other in
   works of charity. When the Catholic church is to be enlarged, a bazaar
   is held by the ladies of the parish, and Mary invites her Episcopalian
   friend to take charge of a booth; which she does. Not long after, a fair
   is given by the Episcopalians to raise money towards the erection of a
   new church. Martha asks Mary to take a booth, and Mary not only does
   so, but even gives some objects to be sold at the fair. At this her Catholic neighbors take scandal. What do you think of Mary's conduct?
8. Read the story of Saul and David. It shows that nothing is so apt to
   deceive us as envy. Saul persuaded himself that David was his enemy.

In reality he was envious because, through his victory over Goliath, David received greater honor from the people than the King. How did David try to make Saul see the injustice of his conduct?

9. *Reading: A Little Meditation on Envy.*—"A neighbor has made a large donation for the support of needy families. Thereupon one remarks: 'He can give; he's got it.' Another: 'That's a great deal; he isn't usually so liberal.' A third: 'He knows why he is so generous.' A fourth: 'In his younger days he used his money for other purposes.' A fifth: 'He wants people to talk about him.' Everyone had some mud to fling at the good deed. Worst of all, not one sees anything malicious in his words, nor suspects that he is laying his own envious heart bare before his fellow men. Such judgments are not heard once in a great while; they are the stock in trade of most men. Let us examine ourselves. Perhaps we shall find that we are no exceptions to the rule."

6. Thou Shalt Not Kill

1. Charity and justice oblige us to respect and safeguard the life and health of our neighbor. How do we injure our neighbor's health?
2. What is meant by murder? Why do we call it a sin that cries to Heaven for vengeance?
3. Give three reasons why murder is such a heinous crime.
4. When is the taking of another's life not murder?
5. Are there any conditions under which one may kill in self-defense? What are they?
6. Has one a right to kill in defense of other goods besides life?
7. May I defend my good name by using physical violence against a detractor or calumniator? If not, what may I do to defend myself?
8. May a woman defend her virtue by taking the life of the aggressor? If so, what justifies her act?
9. Why isn't killing animals murder? Why is cruelty to animals a sin?
10. How do you think murderers should be punished?

7. Thou Shalt Not Steal

1. Make a list of the most common sins against the Seventh Commandment.
2. Distinguish between theft and robbery, usury and interest-taking.
3. Why is one who "corners the market" really a usurer?
4. When is stealing a mortal sin?
5. May a number of small thefts amount to a mortal sin?
6. When an act of injustice has been committed, what is required in order to obtain pardon?
7. On whom does the obligation of restitution fall? Does it fall only on the person who has directly done the injustice?
8. "Losers weepers, finders keepers." Criticize this ancient jingle.
9. "I would rather steal than starve." Comment on these words.
10. *Philip,* a merchant, often travels on the train without paying his fare, giving the conductor a large tip instead. Quite frequently he sells his wares far above their real value, because, he says, others do the same. Sometimes he exaggerates the value of his wares in order to make a sale.

Must Philip make restitution in all these cases? What about the conductor who takes the tips?

8. The Duty of Truthfulness and Fidelity

1. In what does the virtue of Truthfulness consist? The virtue of Fidelity?
2. What is meant by a lie?
3. Distinguish three kinds of lies.
4. What are the most usual motives for lying?
5. Is a deliberate lie ever permissible?
6. If I am allowed to kill in defense of my life, why may I not tell a lie to save my life? (To solve this problem remember that lying is *intrinsically* wrong. That is to say, "it is not wrong merely because it may do harm to another person, but because of itself it violates the moral order." God Himself cannot make a lie right. Killing another is not intrinsically wrong, as is evident from war, hanging and self-defense. Remember also the principle: "The end never justifies the means.")
7. Show that lying is cowardly.
8. What is hypocrisy? Is it as sinful as lying in words? Our Lord calls the hypocrite a "wolf in sheep's clothing"; why?
9. Read Matt. 23, 13-32. Christ denounces the hypocrisy of the Scribes and Pharisees.
10. What is Mental Reservation? When is it lawful? Why should we not make a habit of mental reservation and equivocation?
11. Show that fidelity or trustworthiness is the surest foundation of every relation of man to man. Read carefully Cardinal Faulhaber's praise of fidelity, and comment on his words.
12. The Emperor Marcus Aurelius says in his *Meditations*: "Never esteem anything as of advantage to thee that shall make thee break thy word or lose thy self-respect."

Be Faithful and True.—"In the world of gentlemen and gentlewomen, among the things that stain character and reputation, and close the doors of good society are: a lie, a broken promise, a slander of a woman, an anonymous letter, failure to pay one's debts, cheating at cards, violation of the laws of hospitality by repeating or reporting anything best kept secret learned either as host or as guest."

9. Our Neighbor's Reputation

1. Why must we respect our neighbor's good name?
2. How do we violate this duty?
3. Distinguish between false suspicion and rash judgment. Give examples.
4. Why are calumny and detraction sins against justice as well as against charity? Can these sins be forgiven if we do not do our best to make up for the harm we have done by them?
5. Why is tale-bearing such a detestable sin?
6. *Reading: Imitation of Christ*, Bk. III, ch. 28: "Against the Tongues of Detractors."

Rash Judgment

"O God, I give Thee thanks that I am not like the rest of men, extortioners, unjust, adulterers, nor such as this publican" (Luke 18,11). These are the words of the proud man who, full of his own importance, despises his neighbor, criticizes his behavior and condemns his actions though they be influenced by the purest and most innocent motives. He finds no good in anything except what he says or does himself. You may see him constantly watching the words and actions of his neighbor and upon the least pretext, he blames, judges and condemns without mercy or inquiry. O accursed sin, thou art the cause of enmities, hatred, dissensions, and of eternal damnation of souls!

Tell me, have we any better foundation for judging our neighbor's actions than those persons had who saw the beautiful Judith adorn herself magnificently and visit Holofernes? No, we are no surer of what we see and hear, than were those who saw Potiphar's wife with a piece of Joseph's mantle in her hands, and heard her claim that he had attempted to assault her. Here we have two examples which the Holy Ghost gives us, to show us how deceitful appearances are, and how greatly we sin by forming rash judgments.—St. John Baptist Vianney, Curé of Ars, *Sermons*, p. 228.

CHAPTER IV

Our Duties as Members of the Family, the State, and the Church

1. THE CHRISTIAN FAMILY

"The family," says Pope Leo XIII in one of his great encyclicals, "is the cradle of civil society, and it is largely within the confines of the domestic hearth that is prepared the destiny of nations." By raising marriage to the dignity of a sacrament Christ also sanctified the family, made it the *Christian family*.

1. Authority in the family is vested in the parents.—The husband is the head of the family, the wife its heart and soul. It is only in the Christian family that the wife enjoys that dignity and respect which God originally intended her to have when He made her the companion and helpmate of her husband, not his slave.

2. The duties of parents to their children are embraced in the word *education*. "Education means training, that is, instruction by word and example, by suggestion and direction, by encouragement and repression, by reward and punishment. It means a progressive and well-ordered development of man's three-fold powers, physical, intellectual, and moral. It means the proper formation of the whole man—body, mind, and will." Hence parents are bound

　a) to love their children and to support them until they can support themselves;

　b) to instruct their children in all that is required to enable them to be a success in this life and in the next;

　c) to give them good example by leading a good Catholic life themselves;

　d) to send their children to Catholic schools and, if circumstances oblige them to send them to non-Catholic schools, to safeguard their faith and to see to their religious instruction.

3. The duties of children towards their parents are summed up in the Fourth Commandment in the word *honor*. "Honor thy father and thy mother." Honor embraces three things: reverence, love, and obedience.

　a) *Reverence* is an essentially religious concept. We owe rever-

"And He went down and was subject to them." (Luke 2, 51)

ence in the first place to God, to the Name of God, the house of God, and all things pertaining to God. Now parents share in the creative power of God when they give life to their children, and consequently also in the authority of God over His creatures. Therefore we owe the deepest reverence to our parents all the days of our life. An affront offered to them will be taken as offered to God Himself. "He that feareth the Lord honoreth his parents" (Ecclus. 3,8).

To show dislike or contempt for our parents, or to cause them serious grief, is always sinful; to strike them, or even to threaten to do so, will usually be a mortal sin.

b) Our *love* for our parents is founded on the ties of blood which bind us to them, and is nourished by gratitude for all they have done and do for us. It must be a real internal affection, but it must also show itself in our words and actions, and in our whole conduct. We must be ready to help them in their every need, bear with their faults and weaknesses, never desert them in their lives, and pray for them after their death.

c) The duty of *obedience* flows from the parental authority, without which a happy family life and a successful education of the children is impossible. Children are bound to obey their parents in all that is not sin. Our obedience must be prompt and cheerful; for by obeying our parents we obey God Himself. "Children, obey your parents, for this is pleasing to the Lord" (Col. 3,20).

When the child grows up and leaves the home the duty of obedience ceases. In regard to the choice of a state of life children are not bound to obey their parents, because in this all-important matter each one must follow his own conscience; still, it is a child's duty to seek and consider the advice of its parents before taking such a decisive step.

4. Children are bound to support their parents when through sickness, infirmity, or old age they cannot support themselves. When elder brothers or sisters have begun to work they should throw their earnings into the common fund for the support of the family until they leave home and set up an establishment of their own. The so-called "boarder spirit," so common today, cannot be too deeply deplored.

5. Teachers are put in the place of the parents to educate children in letters and conduct. They therefore share the obligations and the rights of parents. They are, moreover, bound in justice to fulfill the special duties annexed to their office of training the children committed to their charge. The *pupils* are bound to love, reverence, and obey their teachers in all things pertaining to their education.

2. MASTERS AND SERVANTS; WORKMEN AND EMPLOYERS

1. The Duties of Masters and Servants are clearly defined by St. Paul: "Servants, obey in all things your masters according to the flesh, not serving to the eye, as pleasing men, but in simplicity of heart, fearing God. . . . Masters, do to your servants that which is just and equal, knowing that you also have a Master in heaven" (Col. 3,22; 4,1).

2. The Rights and Duties of Workmen and their Employers have been admirably laid down by Pope Leo XIII in his Encyclical on the Condition of the Working Classes (May 15, 1891):

a) Religion teaches the laboring man and the artisan to carry out honestly and fairly all equitable agreements freely entered into; never to injure the property, nor to outrage the person, of an employer.

b) Religion teaches the employers that their work-people are not to be looked upon as their slaves; that in every man they must respect his dignity and worth as a man and as a Christian; that labor is not a thing to be ashamed of, but an honorable calling, enabling a man to sustain his life in a way upright and creditable; and that it is shameful and inhuman to treat men like chattels to make money by, or to look upon them merely as so much muscle or physical power.

c) The employer is bound to see that the worker has time for his religious duties; that he be not exposed to corrupting influences and dangerous occasions.

d) The employer must never tax his work-people beyond their strength, or employ them in work unsuited to their age or sex.

e) The employer must give the workman a fair wage, that is, the wage must be sufficient to support the wage-earner in reasonable and frugal comfort.

f) The employer who grows rich by "sweating" his work-people commits a sin against justice and is bound to make restitution of his ill-gotten goods.

g) It is sometimes the duty of the State to interpose its authority in order to settle labor questions.

h) It is unlawful for workmen to strike when by so doing they violate a *just* and *free* contract. It is wrong to use violence to compel other workmen to strike against their will, or to prevent them accepting work if they desire to do so.

i) If other means of obtaining redress or of securing their rights have failed, it is not wrong for workmen to strike in order to obtain a just wage, or other just, reasonable, and adequate advantage.

3. The Rights and Duties of Citizens

Families naturally form themselves into tribes and nations, and this involves the necessity of a *Government or State*; and so there is another set of rights and duties.

1. The State exists for the sake of the citizens, for their peace and prosperity, for their general temporal welfare. The State, therefore, has the duty "to provide whatever helps and safeguards may be necessary in order that the citizens may be able to develop to the fullest their powers, not only in the physical and material, but also in the intellectual and moral order, and to promote in every legitimate way the public welfare."

As the individual existed before the State, he has rights which the State may not molest, but is bound to respect and to protect always and everywhere. (See the *Declaration of Independence.*)

2. The State, once it is formed, receives its authority from God through the people.—"All power comes from God," says St. Paul. But if the civil power is from God, it is a matter of *religious obligation* to obey its laws, and sinful to transgress them. It is, therefore, false to think that there are any just and valid civil laws which do not bind in conscience, but only under pain of paying the penalty attached. "All human laws, if they are just," says St. Thomas, "have the power to bind in conscience from the Eternal Law of God from which they are derived."

In order to be just and valid a law must not only be made and promulgated by legitimate authority, but it must also be in harmony with the Divine Law; it must serve the common good, and must not be destructive of the inalienable rights of the family and the individual. A law that does not fulfill these requirements is null and void, and cannot bind in conscience.

3. Every citizen is bound to love his country, to show honor, obedience, and loyalty to the constituted authorities, do his share towards the public expense by paying just taxes, and, if necessary, to defend the rights of his country with life and limb.

"Hallowed in the minds of Christians is the very idea of public authority, in which they recognize some likeness and symbol, as it were, of the Divine Majesty, even when it is exercised by one unworthy. A just and due reverence to the laws abides in them, not from force and threats, but from

Titian

THE COIN OF TRIBUTE

a consciousness of duty; for God hath not given us the spirit of fear" (Leo XIII).

4. Voting.—Since citizens have a large share in the election of all public officers from the President to the town marshal, they should fulfill such an important duty faithfully and conscientiously. There may even be a *moral obligation* to vote at elections in order to prevent the election of one who would do grave public harm if elected. If the choice lies between candidates who are equally good or equally bad, there is no obligation in conscience to cast one's vote.

5. Loyalty.—The Church approves all forms of government which answer the needs of human society; but whatever the form be, Catholics should be "foremost in loyalty; slow to criticize their rulers, yet not afraid to do so when necessary; rallying round them at times of crisis; promoting good laws and acting quietly as good citizens who think not only of their own interests, but still more of the general good."

4. Sancta Mater Ecclesia

We are citizens of two commonwealths. By birth or adoption we become citizens of an earthly commonwealth, by Baptism we are born again as subjects of the kingdom of Christ on earth, the Church.

1. Church and State.—The end of the State is, as we have seen, to promote the temporal welfare of its members; to the Church is committed our spiritual and eternal welfare.

"The Almighty has appointed the charge of the human race between two powers, the ecclesiastical and the civil; the one is set over divine, the other over human things. Each in its kind is supreme, each has fixed limits within which it is contained, limits which are defined by the nature and special object of the province of each. Whatever in things human is of a sacred character, whatever belongs to the salvation of souls, or to the worship of God, is subject to the power and judgment of the Church. Whatever is to be ranged under the civil and political order is rightly subject to the civil authority. Jesus Christ has Himself given command that what is Caesar's is to be rendered to Caesar, and whatever belongs to God is to be rendered to God" (Leo XIII).

Hence there should be no friction between the Church and the State.—Their respective spheres are quite distinct, and yet, while keeping within their own boundaries, each can help on and advance the interests of the other. Unfortunately Caesar often demands more than his right.

For three hundred years after the death of Christ the Church and Caesar were in conflict, and countless martyrs died because their consciences bade them "obey God rather than men." Later similar conflicts occurred: with kings and emperors who claimed the right to appoint bishops and to invest them with the insignia of their office; with Protestant princes who claimed the headship of the Church in their lands; with the French Revolutionary Government which trampled under foot the freedom of the Church.

At the present day, too, there are countries, such as Mexico, where the State flagrantly invades the rights of the Church. In others the State claims too much in regard to marriage, and Catholics have to follow the Church against the mandates of Caesar. In others again the government tries to get complete control of education, and thus manifestly exceeds its powers, because education has to do with the *soul* as well as the body.

Against absolute State monopoly of education the Church will ever raise her voice. Such a monopoly not only deprives her of her just rights in the matter of education, but is also a violation of the natural right of parents to educate their children as they see fit—a right explicitly recognized by the Supreme Court of the United States.

2. Our Duties towards the Church.—As a perfect society the Church possesses in the *teaching, priestly,* and *pastoral* office delegated to her by her Divine Founder, the adequate means of attaining her end—the sanctification and supernatural education of her members. Our *duties towards the Church* are defined by this her threefold office.

a) Since the Church has been commissioned by Christ to preserve and teach all revealed truth, we have the duty to accept her teaching, the doctrinal pronouncements of her Head, the Pope, and of the Councils as messages of the infallible God Himself.

b) Since the Church has the right and duty to dispense the mysteries of God, to apply the fruits of the Redemption to individual souls through the Sacraments and the Holy Sacrifice of the Mass, we have the duty to make proper use of the means of grace and salvation offered to us.

c) Since the Church has the power to regulate the religious and moral life of her members by her laws and precepts, we have the duty to submit to her laws and to observe her precepts; to honor those invested with her authority, and to contribute the material means necessary for the efficient administration of their office.

3. Our obedience to the Church must not be the obedience of slaves who fear the lash, but rather the obedience of grateful and loving children. We know that every law of the Church is dictated by her solicitude for our spiritual welfare; hence, even though we do not always see the why and the wherefore of a law, we will nevertheless carry it out loyally and trustingly..

4. As true children of the Church we must take a full share in the life of the Church.—Nothing that concerns her must be indifferent to us. We must play our part in the wonderful drama of her Liturgy, and join zealously in her work for the propagation of the faith at home and abroad; we must follow with real heart-felt sympathy her varying fortunes, her conflicts, sufferings, and triumphs; we must chivalrously enter the lists for her wherever she is outraged by her enemies from without or by traitors in her own bosom.

5. The Catholic loves his Church in spite of the failings and shortcomings which attach to her earthly existence. "Such as she is, she is to him a revelation of the Holiness, Justice, and Goodness of God. The Catholic does not look for an ideal Church, a heavenly Jerusalem on earth. What though his Mother is covered with dust from the long journey; what though her gait is at times slow and weary, and her brow marked with the lines of care and sorrow,—she is his Mother none the less. In her heart there leaps up the old flame of love. Out of her eyes shines the old faith. From her hands stream forth the old blessings unceasingly."

5. The Christian Ideal

The following beautiful prayer, which the Church owes to the saintly Pontiff Clement XI (1700-1721), not only embraces all that is necessary for salvation, but is also an admirable summary of Catholic Ethics and an excellent guide to the attainment of the Christian Ideal:

"O my God, I believe in Thee; do Thou strengthen my faith. All my hopes are in Thee; do Thou secure them. I love Thee; teach me to love Thee daily more and more. I am sorry that I have offended Thee; do Thou increase my sorrow.

"I adore Thee as the Author of my being; I aspire after Thee as my last end. I give Thee thanks as my constant benefactor; I call upon Thee as my sovereign protector.

"Lead me, O my God, by Thy wisdom, restrain me by Thy justice, comfort me by Thy mercy, defend me by Thy power.

"To Thee I desire to consecrate all my thoughts, words, actions, and sufferings; that henceforward I may think of Thee, speak of Thee, refer all my actions to Thy greater glory, and suffer willingly whatever Thou shalt appoint.

"Lord, I desire that in all things Thy will may be done, because it is Thy will, and in the manner that Thou willest.

"I beg of Thee to enlighten my understanding, to inflame my will, to purify my body, and to sanctify my soul. Let me not be infected with pride, allured by flattery, deceived by the world, or ensnared by Satan. Give me grace to keep my memory pure, to restrain my tongue, and to watch over my eyes and all my senses.

"Give me strength, O my God, to expiate my offenses, to overcome temptation, to subdue my passions, and to acquire the virtues proper to my state.

"Fill my heart with tender affection for Thy goodness, hatred of my faults, love of my neighbor, and contempt of the world. Let me always remember to be submissive to my superiors, courteous to my inferiors, faithful to my friends, and charitable to my enemies.

"Assist me to overcome pride by humility, sensuality by mortification, avarice by almsdeeds, anger by meekness, and lukewarmness by devotion.

"O my God, make me prudent in my undertakings, courageous in dangers, patient in affliction, and humble in prosperity.

"Grant that I may be ever attentive at my prayers, temperate at my meals, diligent in my employments, and constant in my good resolutions. Let my conscience be ever upright and pure, my exterior modest, my conversation edifying, and my deportment well-ordered.

"Assist me that I may labor continually to overcome nature, to correspond with Thy grace, to keep Thy commandments, and to work out my salvation.

"Discover to me, O my God, the nothingness of this world, the greatness of Heaven, the shortness of time, and the length of eternity.

"Grant that I may prepare for death; that I may fear Thy judgment, escape Hell, and in the end obtain Heaven through the merits of Jesus Christ our Lord."

SUGGESTIONS FOR STUDY AND REVIEW

I. The Christian Family

1. Pope Leo XIII calls the family "the cradle of Society." Why?
2. Why do we speak of the *Christian* Family?
3. In whom is authority in the family vested? What is the place of the wife?
4. What is meant by Education?
5. Sum up the duties of parents in regard to the education of their children.
6. "Honor thy father and thy mother." What duties does the word "Honor" embrace? Briefly explain each.
7. List some sins against the Fourth Commandment that boys and girls may be guilty of.
8. Describe a child that really loves its parents.
9. Are children bound to obey their parents in regard to choice of a state of life? Explain.
10. When are children bound to support their parents?
11. What are the obligations and rights of Teachers?
12. Name some ways and means of showing reverence, obedience and love to one's teachers.

Filial Piety

St. Monica's Joy at Augustine's Conversion. "Shortly before her death, Monica said to her son Augustine: 'My son, for mine own part I have no further delight in anything in this life. What I do here any longer, and to what end I am here, I know not, now that my hopes in this world are accomplished. One thing there was, for which I desired to linger for a while in this life, and that was that I might see thee a Catholic Christian before I died. My God hath done this for me more abundantly than I had hoped, since I now see you His servant. What do I here?' . . ."

St. Monica's Spiritual Testament. "Scarce five days after, or not much more, she fell sick of a fever: and in that sickness one day she fell into a swoon and was for a while withdrawn from these visible things. We hastened around her; but she was soon brought back to her senses; and looking on me and my brother standing by her, said to us enquiringly, 'Where was I?' And then looking fixedly at us who were overcome with grief, she said: 'Here shall you bury your mother.' I held my peace and kept back my tears. . . . Soon after she said to both of us: 'Lay this body anywhere; let not the care for that in any way disquiet you: this only I request, that you would remember me at the Lord's altar, wherever you be.' And having delivered these sentiments in what words she could, she held her peace, being tormented by her growing sickness."

Augstine's Grief at His Mother's Death. "On the ninth day of her sickness, and the fifty-sixth year of her age, and the three and thirtieth

Schaffer

St. Monica and St. Augustine

of mine, was that pious and holy soul freed from the body. I closed her eyes; and there flowed withal a mighty sorrow into my heart, which was overflowing into tears; mine eyes at the same time, by the violent command of my soul, drank up their fountain wholly dry; and woe was me in such a strife!

Augustine's Comfort. "I found comfort indeed in her testimony, when, in her last illness, mingling her endearments with my acts of duty, she called me her 'dutiful son,' and mentioned with great affection of love, that she never had heard any harsh or reproachful sound uttered by my mouth against her. But yet, O my God, who madest us, what comparison is there betwixt that honor which I paid her, and her slavery for me? Because I had lost such great comfort in her, my soul was wounded, and my life, as it were, rent asunder. . . .

Augustine's Prayer for His Mother. "Laying aside for a while her good deeds, for which I give thanks to Thee, God of my heart, my praise and my life, I do now beseech Thee for the sins of my mother. Hearken unto me, I entreat Thee, by the Healer of our wounds, who hung upon the tree, and now sitting at Thy right hand maketh intercession to Thee for us. I know that she dealt mercifully and from her heart and forgave her debtors their debts; do Thou also forgive her debts, whatever she may have contracted in so many years since the water of salvation had cleansed her. Forgive her, Lord, forgive, I beseech Thee. Enter not into judgment with her. Let Thy mercy be exalted above Thy justice; for Thy words are true, and Thou hast promised mercy unto the merciful. . . .

Augustine Entreats Others to Pray for His Departed Parents. "May she then rest in peace with her husband, before and after whom she never had any; whom she obeyed, with patience bringing forth fruit unto Thee, that she might win him also unto Thee. And inspire, O Lord my God, inspire Thy servants my brethren, Thy sons my masters, whom with voice, and heart, and pen I serve, that so many as shall read these Confessions, may at Thy altar remember Monica Thy handmaid, with Patricius, her husband, through whom Thou broughtest me into this life. May all with devout affection remember my parents in this transitory light, that so my mother's last request of me, may through my Confessions, more than through my prayers, be through the prayers of many more abundantly fulfilled to her" (St. Augustine, *Confessions,* Bk. IX, 10-13).

2. Masters and Servants; Workmen and Employers

1. Copy the text: Col. 3,22; 4,1. What does it tell you about the duties of masters and servants?
2. What does Leo XIII say in his Encyclical *On the Condition of the Working Classes* in regard to the rights and duties of the workman and the employer?
3. Is it ever lawful for workmen to strike?
4. Copy James 5,4. What does it teach the employer?
5. What do you understand by a "living wage"?

3. Rights and Duties of Citizens

1. How did Governments or States arise?
2. What is the purpose of the State?
3. What rights of the individual may the State never interfere with?
4. "All power comes from God," says St. Paul. What follows from this for the State? For the Citizen?
5. Describe a just law.
6. What should be the attitude of the citizen towards a wicked and unjust law?
7. Why do just laws bind in conscience?
8. List five duties of every citizen.
9. Explain: "There may be a moral obligation to vote."
10. Describe a citizen who is loyal to his country.
11. Show how a good Catholic is necessarily always a good citizen.
12. *Reading:* Rom. 13,1-7.

4. Sancta Mater Ecclesia

1. Show that we are citizens of two commonwealths.
2. In what matters are we subject to the power and judgment of the Church?
3. Why should there be no friction between the Church and the State?
4. Why does friction often arise between the Church and the State?
5. Why must the Church oppose absolute monopoly of education by the

State? Is the United States Supreme Court in accord with the Church in this matter?

6. What means does the Church possess to attain the purpose for which she was instituted by Christ?

7. What follows for us (*a*) from the Teaching Power of the Church; (*b*) from the Priestly Power of the Church; (*c*) from the Ruling or Pastoral Power of the Church?

8. Name the Precepts of the Church. To which Power of the Church does each refer?

9. Describe in detail how you should give material and spiritual support to your pastor.

10. Describe the character of the obedience which Catholics owe to the Church and her laws.

11. Explain: "We must take a full share in the life of the Church."

12. Why do we love the Church in spite of the abuses that have always existed and will always exist in her? (Do we renounce citizenship because of the abuses which exist in the State? Or because some Presidents, Governors, Mayors, and other officials are dishonest, cowardly, or immoral? Are not the representatives of the Church as well as those of the State human beings subject to temptation and fall? Is our own life free from blemish? If every member of the Church were perfect, the whole Church would be perfect. Popes, Bishops, and priests are taken from the rank and file of the faithful. Do you pray for the Church, for the Pope, for the Bishops, and the priests? Do you exaggerate their shortcomings? Christ told the people to follow the good doctrine, not the bad example of the Scribes and Pharisees who sat on the Chair of Moses [Matt. 23,1-4]. If a priest told us to do what was wrong, we should have to disobey him; but we have no excuse to disobey him because he may have many faults and failings.)

13. *Readings:*

(*a*) Tilmann Pesch, S. J., *The Christian Philosophy of Life*, pp. 158-169: "What is Christ's Church to us?" (*See below.*)

(*b*) John L. Stoddard, *Rebuilding a Lost Faith*, pp. 216-222: "Some Catholic Privileges and Compensations."

WHAT IS CHRIST'S CHURCH TO US?

Ask the Catholic priest: Who gave you the right to direct me in matters concerning my soul's salvation, to teach me, and to absolve me from my sins? He will point you to his *Bishop*. Ask the Bishop in his turn: Who gave you this right? and he will answer: The *Pope*. Ask the Pope, and he replies: I hold the same power which my predecessor held. Pass up the long line; one after another gives you the same answer, until you come to *Peter*. Ask him: Whence hast thou this authority? He will point to *Christ*, and Christ Himself will make answer: *All power is given to Me in Heaven and on earth.*

He, therefore, who submits himself to the Church, submits to Christ; and he who submits to Christ, submits to God.—Pesch, *The Christian Philosophy of Life.*

Index

NOTES

NOTES

NOTES